CRIMINAL MASTERMINDS

CRIMINAL MASTERMINDS
EVIL GENIUSES OF THE UNDERWORLD

CHARLOTTE GREIG

BARNES & NOBLE
NEW YORK

This 2006 edition published by Barnes & Noble Publishing, Inc.
by arrangement with Arcturus Publishing Limited

M 10 9 8 7 6 5 4 3 2

ISBN-13: 978-0-7607-7574-5
ISBN-10: 0-7607-7574-5

Printed in China

Cover design by Steve Flight
Book design by Beatriz Waller
Layout by Adelle Morris

CONTENTS

INTRODUCTION

Criminals fascinate us. Sometimes the fascination is rooted in terror – as we contemplate monstrous killers and predatory paedophiles. Sometimes it is tinged with admiration – as we remember the Robin Hoods, the outlaws in our midst who broke the rules and got away with it, at least for a time. Sometimes we cannot help but be impressed by the sheer energy and ingenuity of the criminal mind – as we think of the criminal masterminds who, in another life, might easily have become successful business executives.

This book tells the stories of fifty of the most ruthless, most devious and most effective criminals of all time. It includes stories of masterminds like Anthony 'Fats' Pino, who meticulously planned a bank robbery that became known as 'the crime of the century'; and of powerful drug barons, some of them – like Howard Marks – with a moral code of sorts, and others – like the Arellano-Felix brothers – entirely without. Also included are the terrorist masterminds who, in recent years, have struck at the heart of western civilization: from major figures like the elusive Osama bin Laden to desperate, lone individuals such as Ted Kaczynski, known as 'The Unabomber'.

Like a scene from a Hollywood film – the gunned-down 'El Mon' of the Tijuana cartel

From humour to horror

Not all the stories of criminal masterminds are disturbing, however. Some are amusing, because of the sheer cheek of the criminals: in particular, the fraudsters, from Frank 'Catch Me If You Can' Abagnale to Count Victor Lustig, who became famous for 'selling' the Eiffel Tower – twice. Others are exciting, such as the adventures of swashbuckling escape artists like Jack Sheppard and 'Papillon', or outlaws such as Butch Cassidy and Ned Kelly, who became folk heroes as tales of their audacious heists and brave escapes were handed down through history.

Other stories are frankly horrifying, such as those of murderers Charles Manson and Jack Unterweger, who somehow managed to convince impressionable people around them that they were heroes (in Manson's case, his followers actually believed he was a god). These are the cases that raise questions in our minds, not only about the

brutality of psychopaths, but also about the way apparently ordinary people allow themselves to be led into evil, through a mixture of gullibility and a fascination with violence.

Does the end justify the means?

In this book you will read tales of ruthless mobsters, from Al Capone to John Gotti, that set us wondering about the social reasons why bright, talented young men growing up in poverty turn to a life of crime; could it be that, if dealt a different hand of cards in life's game, they might have become players in the legal, corporate world instead of brutal killers in the underworld of crime?

The infamous Charles Manson shaved his head to be more like the Devil

In the same way, the stories of double agents, whether all-American boys like Christopher Boyce and Aldrich Ames or urbane upper-class Britons such as Kim Philby and Anthony Blunt, give us food for thought: were these individuals, all highly intelligent people, essentially acting out of self-interest, or did they feel a sense of moral indignation at what they perceived as their governments' corrupt practices? Was it perhaps that they simply got caught up in a web of lies to such a degree that, in the end, they could no longer tell wrong from right? By the end of these stories, we begin to realize that once human beings – whether individuals or governments – begin to operate on the basis that 'the end justifies the means', in a short time our civilized moral code becomes meaningless.

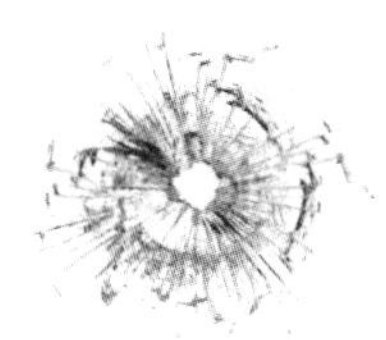

What makes a criminal?

This book explores the lives of these master criminals as we attempt to answer the question: what is it that makes one person of great abilities a hero, and another a criminal? For, in the main, these are stories of talented or charismatic individuals who use their talents in the service of evil rather than good. The question is, why?

In a sense, the answer is obvious. Most criminals – whether stupid or clever – act out of a combination of greed, self-interest and lack of concern for others. The gains – and the risks – are clear enough. As Willie 'The Actor' Sutton allegedly put it, when asked why he robbed banks: 'Because that's where the money is.' However, the picture that emerges from these stories is actually a more complex one.

As one would expect, the social milieu in which criminals grow up usually has a major part to play in their career choice. During the Prohibition period, career opportunities in the legal world were few and far between for immigrant youngsters raised on the mean streets of America's big cities. It is therefore no wonder that the more ambitious and ingenious among them turned to bootlegging, drug running and the like to make their fortunes, rather than spend their lives working for a pittance in the same kind of dead-end jobs as their parents. However, even in this category, there are exceptions. Arnold Rothstein, for example – the man known as 'The Big Bankroll' – was the son of a wealthy New York Jewish businessman, and could easily have chosen from a range of middle-class careers. Why, then, did he choose to become a gangster instead?

George 'Machine Gun' Kelly: for the first time on the legal end of a gun

Perhaps it was for financial gain. Before he met his violent end, Rothstein had become an immensely wealthy man. However, his history shows that there were emotional reasons why he may have chosen to become a gangland criminal rather than a respectable businessman. From an early age, he had been rejected by his parents, and it may be that he later took to crime as a form of rebellion against his family and its culture. Certainly, this trajectory is common enough among criminals from well-to-do families; although here, once again, the picture is not always simple. In some cases, such as that of George 'Machine Gun' Kelly, one cannot help feeling that, no matter what the circumstances, here was a young man bent on a life of violent crime, for whatever reason.

Thrill seekers

If social and emotional pressures play a part, what else makes a criminal mastermind? Intelligence, one might say, but if you analyze a master criminal's career, it becomes clear that, in many cases, these individuals often avoid the most intelligent course of action open to them – to operate within the law, rather than outside it. Clearly, many of them have the brains to make their fortunes legally, or at least to 'go straight' once they have amassed money; but many choose not to do so. What emerges from a lot of these stories is that most high-profile criminals are not simply intelligent people prevented by their social or emotional background from becoming well-to-do citizens. They do not just want money: they want excitement, adventure, the thrill of the chase. They are, in essence, thrill seekers.

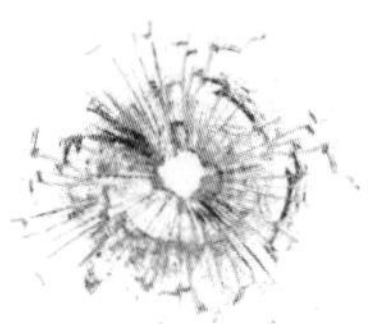

Christopher Boyce, who became a spy and sold secrets to the Russians, put it clearly when he was asked about the motivation for his actions. He said that he believed his government was wrong; that he liked the idea of getting some extra cash; but above all, that he had 'a lust for adventure'. This need for kicks is echoed by many other characters in this book: from drug barons like George Jung to escape artists such as Jacques Mesrine; from terrorists like Carlos the Jackal to fraudsters such as Frank Abagnale Jr. All of them, to a greater or lesser degree, are men and women who enjoy danger, who prefer speeding in the fast lane to cruising safely in the middle of the road. Those who prefer to keep a low profile, who like a quiet life and who invest their ill-gotten earnings cautiously and sensibly as soon as they can, are the exception rather than the rule: perhaps Meyer Lansky and, to a certain degree, Mickey Cohen – both products of the Prohibition era – come into this rare category.

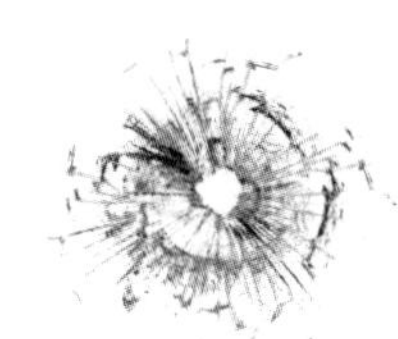

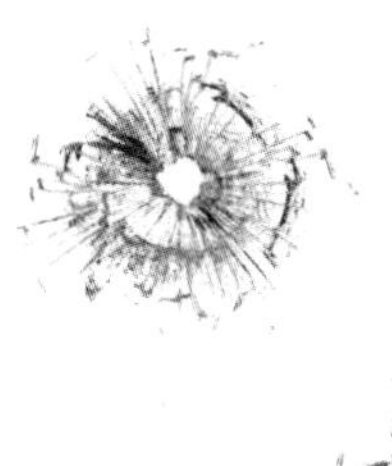

Bloodthirsty killers

As well as the need to take risks, there is another, more disturbing element to the make-up of a criminal mastermind. This is the need for another kind of thrill: that of killing. The obvious examples here are the charismatic killers, men like Charles Manson and Jack Unterweger, who showed signs of more than average intelligence and yet were brutal psychopaths. Then there are the outlaws, such as Bonnie and Clyde, who evidently got their kicks from killing. (Some have argued that Bonnie Parker was not a killer, but she was clearly involved in the murders that took place whether or not she pulled the trigger.) Bloodthirsty drug barons such as Ramon Arellano-Felix and violent mobsters like 'Bugsy' Siegel are also in this category. So are terrorists, such as Abu Nidal or Timothy McVeigh, who cold-bloodedly murdered innocent victims for their own political causes. In fact, there are very few types of master criminals – with the possible exception of fraudsters – who are not involved with violence. Even those who do not have blood on their hands are often responsible, in an indirect way, for violence against others.

In conclusion, it seems that the profile of the criminal mastermind is a complex one. Intelligence plays a part, of course, as does greed; more crucially, however, the need to take risks and the thrill of the chase – of adventure, of danger and of violence – defines the mind of the master criminal. In these fifty stories, you will find out how the master criminals of the past and of the present obeyed that need.

Timothy McVeigh – meticulously planned an attack that rocked the world

RUTHLESS ROBBERS

Planning the perfect heist is the ultimate challenge for the criminal mastermind: the perfect crime is the Holy Grail of the criminal underworld. Few have achieved it, and if they have, it is highly likely that the authorities, and the public, would not know about it as the perfect crime must surely be the one that goes undetected – literally. In most cases, someone slips up or something goes wrong, whether it's a gang member who makes a mistake during the raid, a staff member who behaves in an unpredictable way, a safe that refuses to open, a door that refuses to unlock or – and this is where many bank robbers make their mistake – the way the gang members behave once the raid is over; spending their money a little too freely and attracting attention accordingly. There are many instances in which gangs have meticulously planned every aspect of a robbery and pulled it off successfully, only to come to grief when they relax and begin to spend their loot. Surprisingly, although many bank robbers may show a tremendous degree of intelligence, ingenuity and caution when planning and executing a scam, they seem unable to act with the same degree of focus once the big day is over.

Here, you will find the stories of bank robberies that hit the headlines: from the Brinks Mat Robbery of 1983 to Anthony 'Fats' Pino's textbook raid on a Boston bank in 1950, dubbed 'the crime of the century'. We also look at some of the big names in the bank robbing business, from Ronnie Biggs, the Great Train Robber, to Willie 'The Actor' Sutton, a bank robber whose legendary disguises helped net him a cool two million dollars before he was finally brought to justice.

Jonathan Wild

Jonathan Wild – a criminal disguised as a gentleman. Society took against him when he was found out and the crowd called for blood at his execution

During the late eighteenth century, Jonathan Wild organised crime on a grand scale in London: his illegal operations were complex, but essentially, he ran gangs of robbers and thieves who stole goods, and then returned them to their rightful owners for a reward. His business made him a handsome profit, and he became a well-known public figure, dressing in fine clothes and carrying a silver-topped cane. However, eventually the law caught up with him, and overnight he became a villain, despised by the public and the press who had once lionised him.

A gang of thieves and whores

Born in Wolverhampton in 1683, Wild's family was a poor one. As a small boy, he became apprenticed to a buckle-maker and afterwards worked as a servant. As a young man, he ran up debts and spent time in a debtor's prison, where he met a prostitute named Mary Milliner. When the pair were released, he lived with her and became part of her gang of thieves and whores. During this time, Wild became a pimp and also bought and sold stolen goods. He developed an ingenious scam whereby thieves would let him know what property they had stolen, and victims of theft would also come to him to get their goods back. He took care never to have the stolen goods in his possession, and took a cut from both thieves and victims for his services. He posed as a do-gooder, recovering stolen items from thieves and returning them to their rightful owners, even working with the police to help the victims of theft; but in reality, it was he who was organizing the thefts in the first place.

It was not long before Wild built up a substantial business. His business rapidly expanded,

IONATHAN WILD THIEF-TAKER GENERAL OF GREAT BRITTAIN & IRELAND

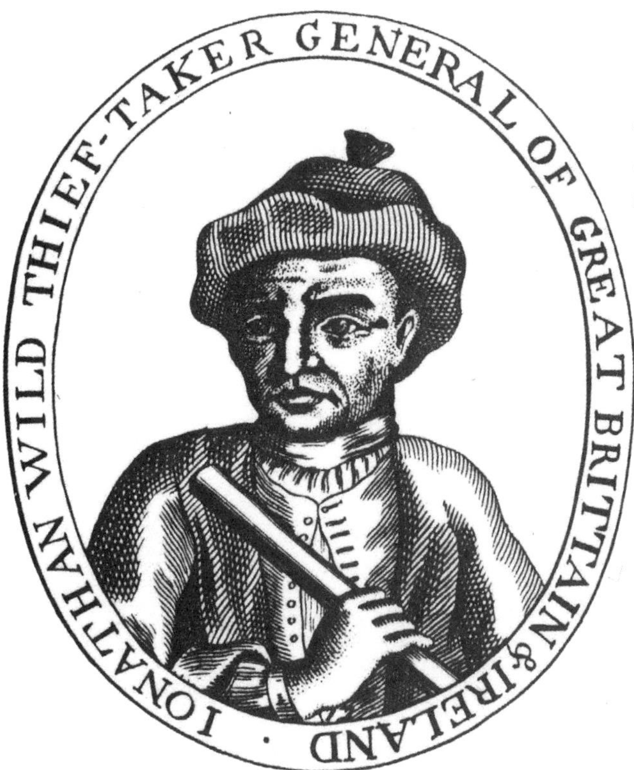

A 'ticket' inviting fellow bad characters to Wild's execution. Having been feted, his fall from grace was a long one

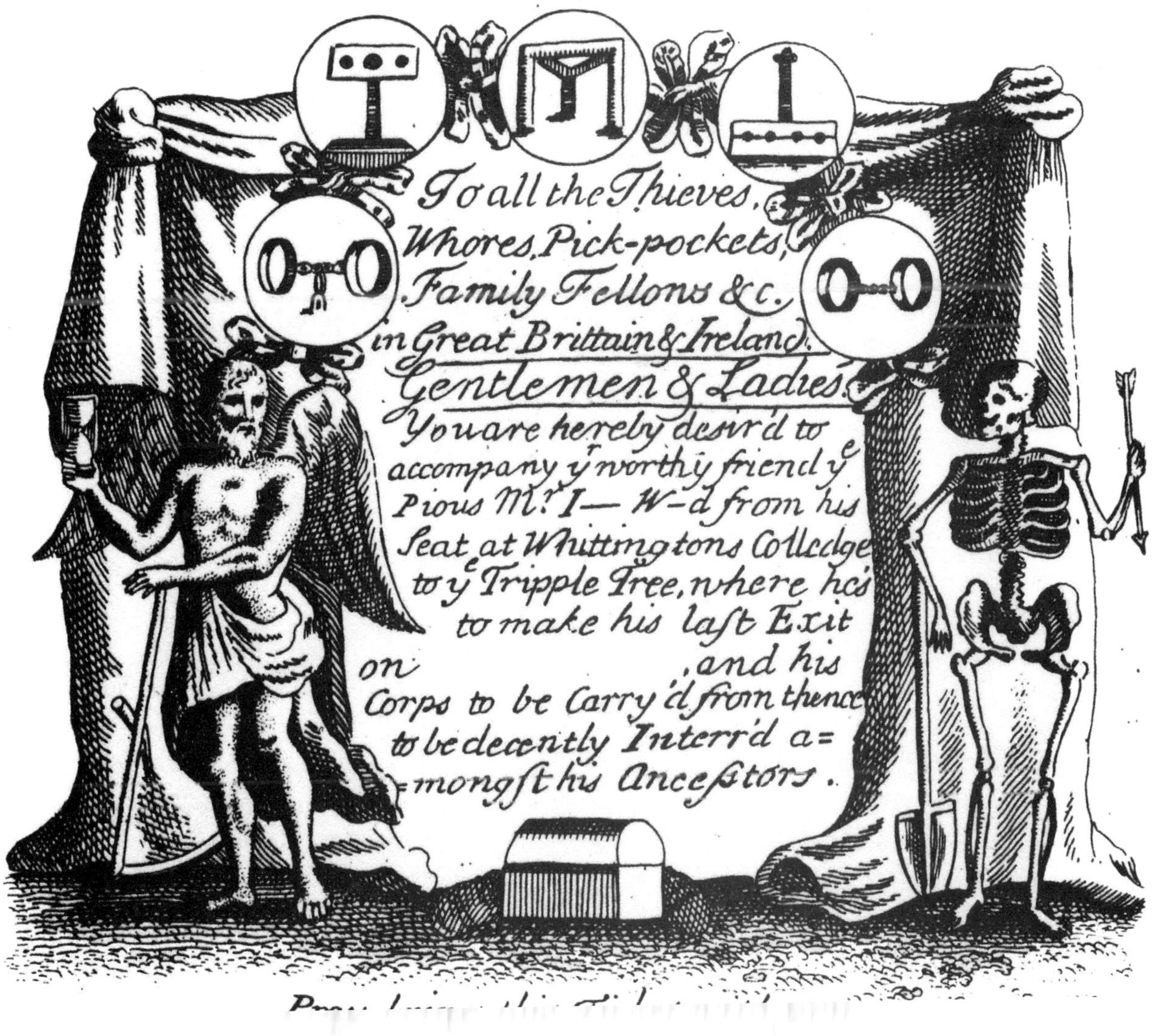

To all the Thieves,
Whores, Pick-pockets,
Family Fellons &c.
in Great Brittain & Ireland.
Gentlemen & Ladies.
You are hereby desir'd to
accompany yr worthy friend ye
Pious Mr. I— W—d from his
Seat at Whittingtons Colledge
to ye Tripple Tree, where he's
to make his last Exit
on , and his
Corps to be Carry'd from thence
to be decently Interr'd a=
=mongst his Ancestors.

Crowds gathered in the streets to pelt him with rotten fruit as he and his jailers made their way to the gallows and, while he was waiting to meet his death, yelled at the executioner to make haste.

and he began to employ jewellers to melt down gold and reset precious stones. In addition, he hired out tools to burglars, and exported stolen goods to Holland in his own ship. He became a well-known, successful public figure, calling himself 'Thief-Taker General of Great Britain and Ireland', and posing as a hero, a man who spent his time catching criminals on behalf of the public.

Double-crossing 'thief-taker'

As crime in London escalated, Wild became more famous. Yet he was secretly running a large gang of thieves, keeping records of their names and their thefts in a ledger. He kept control of his gang by threatening to turn them in to the police; when one of them annoyed him, he would cross their name out in the ledger and send them to the gallows, gaining a reward of forty pounds each time he did so. It is from Wild's practice of betraying his employees and crossing out their names in the ledger that we get the expression 'to double cross'.

By now, Wild had an office at the Old Bailey, London's famous criminal court, where victims would call and miraculously find their stolen goods waiting for them, apparently recovered by Wild's 'thief-takers'. Wild was by now being consulted by the government on how to deter crime in the city, and recommended an increase in the reward for capturing thieves, from forty to a hundred and forty pounds, thereby raising his pay while continuing to maintain his pose as a national hero.

Hanged on the gallows

Eventually, however, his luck ran out. The authorities became aware of what Wild was up to, and in 1718 passed a law informally known as the 'Wild Act', which made it a crime to accept a reward without prosecuting the thief. At first, Wild was able to get around this by asking his clients to leave money for him at a safe house, but in the end he slipped up and was caught taking a reward fee. He was convicted of the crime and sentenced to be hanged.

The public was furious when it found out that, instead of being a respected public servant, Wild had actually been organizing crime in London on a grand scale. Crowds gathered in the streets to pelt him with rotten fruit as he and his jailers made their way to the gallows and, while he was waiting to meet his death, yelled at the executioner to make haste. A story that went down in legend has it that before Wild died, he made one last typical and flamboyant gesture: he picked the executioner's pocket.

Brinks Mat Robbers

The Brinks Mat Robbery, which took place on 26 November 1983, is one of the most famous in criminal history. The sheer quantity of the haul – several tons of gold, worth about twenty-six million pounds sterling – made it the biggest robbery ever to take place in Britain. What makes the robbery even more extraordinary is that, to this day, a great deal of the gold has never been recovered. Some of it was melted down and mixed with copper to make it untraceable and some found its way, through the criminal underworld, into private foreign bank accounts in the West Indies and Switzerland. Not only that, but it is also thought that many people connected to the robbery continue to live a life of luxury. For all these reasons, the Brinks Mat Robbery remains a mystery, one that the police and the authorities will probably never entirely solve.

To get away with such an enormous quantity of gold seems an incredible feat, yet the truth is that the Brinks Mat Robbers never planned the heist on such a large scale. Originally, the plan was for the robbers to steal three million pounds sterling in cash. However, when they broke into the Brinks Mat warehouse at Heathrow Airport they found a little more than they were expecting: 6,800 bars of pure gold, packed into 76 boxes, waiting to be taken to the Far East.

John Palmer was acquitted of charges of handling the stolen Brinks Mat gold. It has been said that all gold jewellery sold in the UK since the robbery is partly composed of Brinks Mat bars

A stash of gold bullion

The gang was a well-organized group of six south London armed robbers. Through a family connection with a security guard who worked at the warehouse, the robbers had insider knowledge of the interior of the building, and knew of a safe within it that was stashed with large quantities of cash. On the night of the robbery, the six men broke into the warehouse, terrorizing the security guards by pouring petrol over them and threatening to set them alight with matches unless they revealed the combination numbers of the safe. (The security guard known to the robbers had phoned in sick that evening, an action that later aroused a great deal of suspicion.)

Under pressure, the guards told the intruders the combination for the safe. However, the gangsters were in for a surprise. When they opened the safe, instead of finding wads of cash, they found it full of gold bullion. Undaunted, the

Squeaky clean? Gordon Parry was tried as a money-launderer for the Brinks Mat robbers – one of the drawbacks of the unexpected windfall of gold was how to process it without attracting attention

thieves decided to steal the whole lot. What should have been a smash'n'grab raid ended up taking about two hours, as the robbers found themselves having to organize a bigger getaway vehicle to cope with the heavy stash of gold upon which they had stumbled. Amazingly, given the time it took to complete the robbery, the gang got clean away that night.

However, such a large amount of gold bullion was not easy to hide. Before long, police were on the case of two well-known south London armed robbers, Brian Robinson, known as 'The Colonel', and Mickey McAvoy. Both men had been living in ordinary working-class houses in London before the robbery, but had suddenly moved to a mansion in nearby Kent. They had apparently paid for the property in cash. It was also believed that they had acquired two Rottweiler dogs named 'Brinks' and 'Mat'.

'The Fox'

Robinson and McAvoy may have been experienced armed robbers, but neither was a particularly astute criminal. As it later emerged, in order to dispose of the gold, the pair had called in an underworld character with a little more finesse than they themselves possessed. This person was known as 'The Fox'. The Fox, in conjunction with a jeweller called Solly Nahome, had arranged for the gold to be melted down into smaller goods. In this way, Robinson and McAvoy hoped to escape detection.

However, in planning the robbery, they had made some elementary mistakes. Police were now on the trail of Anthony Black, the security guard who had given the gang inside information about the safe. It did not take long

When they broke into the Brinks Mat warehouse at Heathrow Airport they found a little more than they were expecting: 6,800 bars of pure gold.

to find out that Black was Brian Robinson's brother-in-law. Under pressure from the police, Black soon gave evidence against the gang, which resulted in a prison sentence of twenty-five years each for Robinson and McAvoy. Black himself received a six-year sentence, of which he served three years, for providing the robbers with a key to the main door and for divulging the details of the warehouse's layout.

Tracking down the culprits

The main culprits in the robbery were now in prison, but it soon became clear that the gold itself would be hard to recover. Much of it was now circulating in different forms, as jewellery or mixed with copper so that it was impossible to trace. A man named Kenneth Noye, who had experience in the gold smelting trade, had been brought in to help mask the gold's origins in this way.

From Spain to Costa Rica and eventually Florida, John Fleming, aka 'Goldfinger', did his best to avoid answering questions about his possible involvment with the robbery

Brian Perry was also accused of involvement with the case. He was subsequently the victim of a gangland killing

Noye may have been a clever operator in the gold smelting trade, but – like McAvoy and Robinson – as a criminal, he was not exactly subtle in his actions. His first mistake was to open a bank account in Bristol, withdrawing enormous amounts of money from one single branch, so much that the branch had to request extra funds from the Bank of England. Attention was soon drawn to Noye, and he was placed under police surveillance. When Noye discovered DC John Fordham in his garden working undercover, he stabbed the detective to death. Brought to trial in 1985 for the murder, Noye managed to convince the jury that he was innocent, and had acted in self-defence. The following year, however, Noye was in court once more, this time because several gold bars had been found at his house. This time, he received a huge fine and a fourteen-year prison sentence.

In 1996, Noye hit the headlines once more. His vicious temper had again got him into trouble. In an incident of road rage, he had killed motorist Stephen Cameron in front of Cameron's fiancée. After a long hunt, Noye was finally captured, and received a life sentence for the senseless murder.

Over a long period, Noye's stash of gold was eventually found, but to this day a large amount of the Brinks Mat bullion has yet to be recovered. Some believe that it never will be. It is even said that all gold jewellery sold in the UK since the robbery is partly composed of Brinks Mat bars. Whatever the case, the combination of skill, cunning and remarkable stupidity on the part of the robbers and their associates make this one of the most fascinating heists in criminal history.

Gold handler and double murderer Kenneth Noye, now in prison for life

The Great Train Robbers

The Great Train Robbery of 1963 is one of the most famous crimes in British history. A gang of fifteen London criminals hijacked a train and stole over two million pounds sterling in used banknotes; the same amount today would be equivalent to about forty million pounds. However, it was not only the huge amount of money stolen that ensured their notoriety: the heist was also seen by many sections of the popular British press as a highly romantic, flamboyant act on the part of the London underworld. In particular, gang member Ronnie Biggs came to be regarded as a swashbuckling figure who had flouted the authorities and got away with it. One central feature of the robbery that appealed to the public was that no guns were used – although, in actual fact, the robbery was a violent crime, since the train driver was hit over the head with iron bars and was permanently injured. This unpleasant reality was, in some quarters, conveniently forgotten, and in time the train robbers became working-class heroes who were regarded with a great deal of affection by the British public.

Planning the heist

The gang was led by a man named Bruce Reynolds, who planned the operation from the beginning. He was an antiques dealer who drove an Aston Martin, and liked to flash his money around. The front man for the gang was John Wheater, a solicitor with an upper-class background who rented the farmhouse where the gang hid after the heist. Next was Buster Edwards, an ex-boxer turned con man, later immortalized by Phil Collins in the film Buster. Other gang members included Charlie Wilson, a bookmaker, and two big men known as Gordon Goody and Jimmy Hussey, the brawn of the operation. Last, but not least, was the youngest member of the gang, Ronnie Biggs, who as yet had little experience of criminal life.

The operation was meticulously planned, using information about the times large amounts of cash were carried on postal trains going in and out of London. A quiet site outside Cheddington, in Buckinghamshire, was selected, so that the robbers could flag down the train and bag the money without attracting too much attention. The site was also chosen because it was near a military base, where large supply vehicles often travelled around. In this way, the robbers hoped that their movements would not arouse suspicion.

Attacked with iron bars

On 8 August 1963, a few minutes after three o'clock in the morning, the raid began. Wearing railway workers' overalls, the gang rigged up some temporary signals on the line, using batteries for power. Seeing the red 'stop' light ahead, the driver brought the train to a halt. When it stopped, a fireman, David Whitby, got out to find out what the trouble was. Whitby was pulled off the track by Buster Edwards and, once he realized that a robbery was in progress, did not try to resist. However, when the driver, Jack Mills, then got off, other members of the gang attacked him with iron bars, causing him to bleed from the head. Mills collapsed on the side of the track.

More mistakes were made as the train robbers began to panic. The gang included a retired train driver, brought in by Ronnie Biggs to move the train into position so that the mailbags could be easily dropped off. However, the elderly train driver did not understand the workings of modern trains, and was unable to move the stopped train. The injured Mills, still bleeding, was forced to take over and drive the train into position. The gang then formed a human chain to unload over a hundred sacks of money, and made their getaway.

Rounding up the gang

The gang hid out at a nearby farmhouse, Leatherslade Farm. Here, they drank cups of tea and played the board game Monopoly, allegedly using the real banknotes from their haul as money. This activity proved to be their downfall. By the time the police reached the farmhouse,

The Great Train Robbers reunited in 1978, fifteen years on from their heist. The notorious Ronnie Biggs had settled in Brazil, and was at this time making a film with the Sex Pistols

the gang had scattered, but they had left incriminating fingerprints on the Monopoly board and elsewhere. In this way, police were able to identify the men, many of whom were known criminals.

Eventually, thirteen of the fifteen gang members were apprehended and brought to justice. Bruce Reynolds spent five years on the run before the police finally caught up with him. He was then tried and received a prison sentence, of which he served ten years. Buster Edwards fled to Mexico but later gave himself up. Charlie Wilson made a daring escape from prison while serving his sentence, and lived quietly outside Montreal, Canada, for a time until police traced him via a telephone call his wife made to her parents in England. Biggs also made a dramatic

Ronnie Biggs with his long-time girlfriend and eventual wife, Raimunda Nascimento de Castro, in 1974

Ronnie in his later years in Brazil. Despite living the good life there, when his health began to fail he returned to England and arrest

escape from jail, after serving over a year of his sentence. He underwent plastic surgery, travelled around the world and then settled in Rio de Janeiro, Brazil.

They drank cups of tea and played the board game Monopoly, allegedly using the real banknotes from their haul as money.

The later years

In his later years, Biggs became notorious as the one Great Train Robber to avoid capture – even though his initial role in the robbery had been a small one. However, in his later years he became ill, having suffered several strokes, and grew tired of living abroad. He announced his intention to come back to Britain, even if he risked being imprisoned in his bad state of health. When he returned, he was duly apprehended and today continues to serve out his sentence in prison.

In the end, most of the Great Train Robbers were brought to justice. However, the money stolen in the robbery was never recovered. Thus, the Monopoly players of the gang may have collected their money, but they did not pass 'Go' – instead, they went straight to jail.

Anthony 'Fats' Pino

Anthony 'Fats' Pino was the mastermind behind the Great Brinks Robbery. Carried out in Boston on 17 January 1950, this was a minutely planned, audacious bank robbery that was later dubbed the crime of the century. The gang, led by Pino, got away with nearly three million dollars, which was an extraordinary sum for the time. For years, too, it appeared that they had got away with it: there were virtually no clues left at the scene, and the team avoided all the usual pitfalls of being seen spending their mysteriously acquired wealth. Instead, all eight of the men involved agreed that none of them would touch the loot for six years, by which time all memory of the crime would have long receded. This was a classic crime of the sort normally only seen in the movies, a heist carried out by seasoned professionals with meticulous planning and rigorous discipline – a scam that worked like clockwork – and at its heart were the organizational talents of Anthony 'Fats' Pino.

The criminal life

Anthony Pino was born in Italy in 1907, but was brought to the US by his parents while still a young child. Growing up in Boston, he soon gravitated to the criminal life, specializing in burglary. In 1928 he was convicted of sexual abuse of a minor, and in 1941 he was sentenced to prison for breaking and entering with intent to commit a felony and for having burglary tools in his possession. At that point, the Immigration and Naturalization Service initiated proceedings to deport him, having discovered that he had never become a naturalized citizen.

In the late summer of 1944, he was released from the state prison and taken into custody by immigration authorities. He fought against this and, because part of the justification for deporting him was his criminal record, he appealed for a pardon in the matter of the burglary conviction. His appeal was successful and, in September 1949, the authorities agreed to drop the deportation proceedings.

They may, of course, have looked at matters differently had they known that Pino was in the midst of planning the largest bank robbery ever carried out in the US at that time.

Planning the perfect scam

Pino had begun a year before by identifying his target, the new Brinks building in Boston. He then assembled the core members of the team – Joseph 'Specs' O'Keefe, Joseph 'Big Joe' McGinnis and Stanley 'Gus' Gusciora. The gang staked out the building, learning in minute detail the routines of its workforce. Pino discovered that, in the evenings, Brinks employees on the second floor would count the money collected from customers that day. It was a huge amount. The only question was how to get to the second floor: there were at least five locked doors to pass through, and alarms.

Pino came up with a simple but effective plan that just needed immense patience. Over a period of months, the team would frequent the building and identify the locked doors they needed to get through. Each time one of the doors was left open and unattended during daylight hours, one of the gang would remove the central chamber of the lock, take it to a compliant locksmith who would cut a key to fit it, then return the cylinder to the door before anyone realized it was missing. Eventually, the team had keys to all five doors.

All eight of the men involved agreed that none of them would touch the loot for six years, by which time all memory of the crime would have long receded.

Next, they had to wait for the perfect time to strike: when they knew that the take would be high; that there were only a few employees on the premises; and that the surrounding area was quiet. So disciplined was the team in this regard that six times they called off the operation at the very last moment. Finally, on the evening of 17 January 1950, they struck.

Halloween masks

They donned clothing outwardly similar to the Brinks uniform, with navy suits and chauffeur's caps. In addition, they wore rubber Halloween masks, gloves and rubber-soled shoes. At 6.55 pm, while Pino and driver Banfield waited in the car, seven men entered the building.

With their copied keys, they gained access to the second floor, binding and gagging five Brinks employees who were storing and counting money. They carefully loaded up all the money and valuables available. At one point, they were interrupted by the sound of the door buzzer. Horrified, the gang looked out of the window to see a Brinks employee at the door. However, before they could get downstairs and attempt to subdue him, he left, apparently unconcerned. They gang went back to loading up the loot. Within half an hour, they were ready to go.

As soon as the robbers had left, an employee called the police. Minutes later, the police arrived, and were soon joined by FBI agents. There were virtually no clues on the scene: each robber's face had been completely concealed behind a mask and the only physical evidence was the rope and adhesive tape used to bind and gag the employees, and a chauffeur's cap that one of the robbers had left at the crime scene.

The FBI learned that, as well as money, four revolvers had been taken by the gang. The descriptions and serial numbers of these weapons were carefully noted in case they might provide a link to the men responsible for the crime. All the police and the FBI had to go on at this stage was the certainty that the crime had been carried out by professionals, men who would already be known bank robbers. Men like career criminal Anthony Pino.

Strangely enough, all these suspects turned out to have clear alibis for the evening in question. Desperate now, the investigators roamed ever wider. Even old-time criminal outfits like the 'Purple Gang' of the 1930s, and another gang that had specialized in hijacking bootlegged whiskey in the Boston area during Prohibition, became the subjects of inquiries.

The crime of the century

Public interest was immense. The Brinks case was called the crime of the century by the newspapers. Brinks offered a hundred thousand dollar reward for information leading to the arrest and conviction of the persons responsible. Soon the police were deluged with tip-offs from hopeful bounty hunters but were no closer to finding the actual criminals, or at least no nearer to proving their culpability – for many police already had their suspicions as to which local robbers were capable of such an audacious sting.

Suspicions grew stronger when one of the revolvers used in the robbery was found by children on a sand bar at the edge of the Mystic River in Somerville. Then the remains of the truck the gang had used were found in Stoughton, Massachusetts. Two of the gang members in the Brinks Robbery, Specs O'Keefe and Gus Gusciora, lived in Stoughton. Local officers searched their homes, but no evidence linking them with the truck or the robbery was found.

In June 1950, however, both men were arrested in connection with some entirely separate burglaries. They were both sentenced to prison and, while they were inside, rumours started to circulate that O'Keefe had been asking certain other criminals on the outside for money to help with his defence. The police tried hard to drive a wedge between O'Keefe and his fellow robbers but failed. However, once O'Keefe was released in 1955, a rift did indeed develop. O'Keefe accused the others of cheating him out of his money and Pino responded by hiring a hit man to kill him. The hit man in question, Elmer 'Trigger' Burke, shot O'Keefe several times with a machine gun but failed to kill him. In hospital, O'Keefe finally agreed to testify against his fellow gang members.

On 12 January 1956, the FBI arrested Anthony Pino along with several other members of the gang. Gusciora died before he could stand trial. The trial began on 12 August 1956. Eight of the gang received maximum life sentences; O'Keefe received only four years and was released in 1960. Most of the money, however, was never recovered.

Fats Pino nearly planned and pulled off the perfect heist, but was arrested when a fellow gang member agreed to testify against him

Willie 'The Actor' Sutton

Willie Sutton was the nearest thing real life has produced to the kind of bank robber you see in the movies. Most bank robbers are brutal, unimaginative types. Willie Sutton, by contrast, was charming and funny, a snappy dresser and a ladies' man. He used cunning and nerve rather than brute force to pull off his scams. In a thirty-year career during the first half of the twentieth century, he robbed over a hundred banks and netted an estimated two million dollars, an enormous sum for the times.

Willie Sutton was born into an Irish family in Brooklyn, New York, on 30 June 1901, the fourth of five children. He stayed in school until the eighth grade, then left home and got a job. At various times he worked as a clerk, a driller and a gardener, never staying in any one job for more than eighteen months. This was because he had already found his true vocation – as a thief. He started stealing when he was nine or ten, graduating to breaking and entering in his late teens, when he robbed his girlfriend's father's business so that the pair of them could elope.

The birth of the actor

Sutton received a brief prison sentence for this but refused to be discouraged. A veteran safe-cracker called Doc Tate introduced him to the world of professional crime, robbing banks and jewellers. Before long, Sutton was also an expert safe-cracker.

Being able to crack a safe was useful, but it did not solve the question of how to gain access in the first place. Initially, Sutton went along with the traditional approach of storming a bank waving a gun. Then one day, while staking out a bank, he watched uniformed guards get out of an armoured truck and make their way into the bank to collect the day's takings. It was then that he had a brainwave. He realized that if you are wearing the right uniform, no one really looks at your face too hard or asks many questions. He resolved that in the future, rather than storm into a bank, he would disguise himself as a security guard – or mailman or whatever – and gain access that way. As he later recalled, 'that afternoon, "Willie the Actor" was born'.

It was a stunningly effective ploy. One day he would rob a Philadelphia bank in the guise of a mailman; another day it would be a Broadway jewellery store and he would be impersonating a postal telegraph messenger. Other favourite disguises included a policeman and a maintenance man. Along with the disguises, Sutton cultivated a gentlemanly approach. He was polite to his victims. He carried a gun, but prided himself on never having to use it. One victim said that the experience of being caught up in one of his robberies was like being at the movies, except that the usher had a gun.

The great escapes

Sutton spent his ill-gotten gains on fast living and expensive clothes. He married for the first time in 1929, but his wife divorced him after he was finally caught and sentenced to thirty years in jail. He was sent to the much feared Sing Sing Prison. However, the same ingenuity that had made him such a successful bank robber also helped him to become a highly skilled prison escapee. His first escape was on 11 December

1932, when he scaled the prison wall using a pair of nine-foot ladders joined together.

Outside, Sutton went straight back to robbing banks. One particularly audacious raid was on the Corn Exchange Bank and Trust Company in Philadelphia, Pennsylvania, on 15 January 1934. A month later, the police caught up with him again. This time he was sentenced to serve twenty-five to fifty years in Eastern State Penitentiary, Philadelphia. There, he continued to make escape attempts. Four attempts were foiled. Finally, on 3 April 1945, Sutton was one of twelve convicts who escaped through a tunnel. However, he was recaptured the same day by Philadelphia police officers.

For his part in the escape, Sutton's sentence was increased to life imprisonment and he was transferred to the Philadelphia County Prison, Homesburg, Pennsylvania. On 10 February 1947, Sutton and other prisoners dressed as prison guards and carried two ladders across the yard to the wall after dark. As the prison's searchlight surveyed the yard, it lighted on Sutton and his companions. Sutton called out 'It's okay' and the searchlight operator let him carry on. This time, he got clean away.

Media furore

After three more years of bank robberies, Sutton's notoriety had grown to the point that the FBI put him on their list of 'Ten Most Wanted Fugitives'. Cleverly, the FBI noted Sutton's love of high-quality tailoring and his photo was circulated not only to police departments but also to New York tailors. This tactic paid off when Arnold Schuster, a 24-year-old tailor's son,

He carried a gun, but prided himself on never having to use it. One victim said that the experience of being caught up in one of his robberies was like being at the movies.

recognized Sutton on the New York subway on 18 February 1952. Schuster told the police, who later arrested Sutton.

Sutton's arrest provoked a media furore. He had gained a reputation as something of a Robin Hood figure (though while he robbed the rich, he certainly never gave to the poor), and was famous for answering the question 'Why do you rob banks?' with the immortal line: 'Because that's where the money is.' The furore had an unfortunate effect for Schuster. Two weeks later, he was murdered by mob assassins determined to let the public know that turning in wanted criminals was a dangerous pastime.

Sutton was sent to Attica Prison to serve his outstanding life sentence plus a hundred and five years. Now in his fifties, Sutton was unable to escape from Attica and remained there until 1969, when he managed to persuade the authorities that he was seriously ill. On Christmas Eve, he was released from Attica State Prison. The following year, he cheekily made a television commercial to promote a new photo credit card for a bank. He then retired to Florida where he wrote an autobiography full of entertaining tales and the disappointing revelation that the 'that's where the money is' line was actually made up by a journalist. He died in Florida on 2 November 1980 at the age of seventy-nine.

Sutton took another route altogether when robbing banks, preferring to gain access to banks by, quite literally, sheer bare face rather than masked and with a gun

DEVIOUS DRUG BARONS

The exporting and importing of illegal drugs is one of the most rapidly expanding businesses in the world today. On every level – from the lowliest drug runner to the top baron living in luxury – there are big profits to be made. It is therefore no wonder that some of the best minds in the criminal world have devoted themselves to this area of operations. However, there is an extraordinary range of people who run the business. On the one hand, there are those who rule their empires with a mixture of brutality, violence and terror: men like the legendary Pablo Escobar and the Arellano-Felix brothers, who appear to be motivated only by money; while on the other, there are the urbane, apparently peace-loving figures such as George Jung and Howard Marks, whose involvement seems to stem from the hedonism and youthful idealism of the counter-culture of drugs.

On the face of it, these two types of drug baron could not be more different; look more closely, however, and the boundaries between them begin to blur. For example, Escobar, despite his reputation as a cold-blooded murderer, put a great deal of his money into social improvements, including welfare programmes and new housing; Jung, meanwhile, who eschewed violence of any kind and was known for his easy-going temperament, ended up tolerating murder and violence as part of the everyday life of a gangster. What emerges from the stories of these men is that the violence endemic to the illegal drugs business cannot help but corrupt even those who start out with the most positive of motives.

Pablo Escobar

During the 1970s and 1980s, the illegal drugs industry expanded massively in size. What had once been a very marginal industry, selling only to those on the fringes of society, now became a multi-billion dollar business selling to everyone from bankers and politicians to suburban teenagers. The drug at the heart of this expansion was cocaine. The marijuana industry remained relatively small, due to the ease of growing and preparing the product. Cocaine, however, is the product of a particular climate and needs a larger scale production system to process it.

The prime sources of the coca leaf are in South America. For years, cocaine had been manufactured in small quantities and sold at a high price. During the 1970s, however, demand began to build and a few criminal masterminds in South America saw that there were huge profits to be made if they began to control not just the growing, but also the refinement, distribution and sale of cocaine on a much larger scale. Chief among these criminals was a Colombian called Pablo Escobar, who in little more than a decade would become the first of the billionaire drug dealers.

The Medellin cartel

Escobar was born on a small farm in Rionegra, near Medellin in Colombia, on 12 January 1949. In his teens he gravitated towards petty crime. He stole gravestones, of all the unlikely commodities, for resale. He also helped steal cars. Before long, he became involved with a small Mafia-run cocaine-producing operation, and then developed his own small business. He soon became aware that this was a business with an almost limitless market. He approached other cocaine growers in the Medellin area and offered to pay them double what they were receiving for their crop from the Mafia, who were their main buyers. They agreed. He used friends and relatives to take the drugs into the United States and establish distribution networks.

Escobar's business grew with extraordinary speed. His business plan mimicked that of legitimate multinational companies. There were a whole host of separately run cocaine operations – franchises if you like – all manufacturing and distributing cocaine, and all wired into a network that was organized by Escobar to give him a handsome share of their profits. The organization became known as the Medellin cartel, with Escobar its CEO.

To ensure his continued dominance in an incredibly competitive and murderous world – a big business regulated not by law but by machine guns – Escobar used an individual mixture of extreme brutality and surprising philanthropy.

The Colombian necktie

Escobar himself was a hands-on leader who carried out many murders personally. He was

Escobar took on the Mafia and won, building a huge cocaine-based empire in little more than a decade. He is shown here attending a soccer game in 1983, in Medellin, where he sponsored a team

even credited with inventing the 'Colombian necktie' – this referred to his predilection for cutting his victims' throats, then pulling their tongues through the open wound. At the same time as terrorizing his enemies, Escobar ploughed a lot of his ill-gotten money into social improvements. He built sports facilities and new housing, and even created Colombia's first ever welfare programme in his home town. These charitable acts made him an enormously popular figure in Medellin. He was even elected to a seat in Congress in 1982. A useful side effect was that his popularity made it very difficult for rival cartels to assassinate him.

His political career did not last long, but his criminal career continued to flourish. The US appetite for cocaine continued to grow, entirely unaffected by Nancy Reagan's 'Just Say No' campaign. By the late 1980s, Forbes magazine ranked Escobar as the seventh richest man in the world, worth over three billion dollars.

Assassination attempts

By 1989, however, the US started to put extreme pressure on the Colombian government to clamp down on the cocaine moguls; the billions at stake also meant that there were other criminal gangs – in particular the Cali cartel – determined to murder Escobar and take his business.

After several near-miss assassination attempts, Escobar decided on a novel survival plan. In 1990 he turned himself in to the government and agreed to plead guilty to a relatively minor drug-dealing charge for which he would receive an agreed sentence of nine years. What Escobar was able to demand in return for this is remarkable. Firstly, he received a guarantee that he would not be extradited to the United States as the US government wanted. Secondly, he would build his own private prison in which to serve his time. The prison itself, nicknamed the 'Cathedral', was a luxurious fortified abode designed less to imprison Escobar than to keep his enemies out.

Walking out of jail

After a year, Escobar tired of his imprisonment. He was worried that changes in the government might change his terms of imprisonment, and his erstwhile minions were taking advantage of his absence to siphon off huge amounts of money. So in 1991, he went back to running his organization from a succession of safe houses.

Escobar had been right to fear the change in government policy. For the first time, the authorities began to make serious attempts to put an end to his reign. On 2 December 1993, he was trapped in a Medellin apartment block by the secret police, who killed him during a rooftop gun battle. However, his legacy remained: the worldwide trafficking of cocaine continued to expand at full speed.

At the same time as terrorizing his enemies, as his profits began to spiral into the multi-millions, Escobar ploughed a lot of his money into social improvements.

The Arellano-Felix Brothers

Brothers Benjamin and Ramon Arellano-Felix jointly led one of the most successful and bloodthirsty criminal organizations of all time. During the 1990s, they came to dominate the enormously lucrative trade in smuggling drugs – primarily cocaine but also marijuana and amphetamines – into the United States.

Mexico has long been a crucial staging point for drug traffickers thanks to its geographical position. To the south lie the drug-producing countries – particularly the cocaine Mecca that is Colombia – while to the north there are a thousand miles of borderland with the target market, the US. This proximity had long led to any number of small-scale smuggling operations. In the 1990s, however, these organizations came under centralized control, dominated by drug-smuggling cartels. The Arellano-Felix organization became the most brutal and feared of all these cartels.

El Min and El Mon

The Arellano-Felix brothers grew up in the coastal province of Sinaloa, near Mazatlan. Their uncle, Miguel Angel Felix Gallardo, ran a drug-trafficking business out of Tijuana, farther up the west coast, next to the US border. Before long, the four Arellano-Felix brothers – Benjamin, Ramon, Eduardo and Javier – headed north to work for their uncle. They began by smuggling electronic goods – televisions and so forth – and soon graduated to narcotics. In 1989, Gallardo was arrested and the brothers quickly moved to take over the drug route.

Now that they were in charge, the brothers – in particular Benjamin, the oldest and the natural leader – saw the opportunity for all-out expansion. Their skills were a classic mix for Latin American drug barons – a lethal mixture of ingenuity and brutality. Benjamin was the brains of the operation, a mild-mannered man who could pass for an accountant. His youngest brother, Ramon, was unquestionably the leader when it came to brutality. The two brothers nicknamed each other El Min (Benjamin) and El Mon (Ramon).

The organization the Arellano-Felix brothers built up was known locally as the Tijuana cartel, after the dangerous border town in which they were based. However, the field of operation soon expanded to cover a hundred-mile stretch of the border between Tijuana and Mexicali. The brothers would send their drugs by boat or by car. They also used a secret tunnel. At one stage, the US authorities, acting on a tip-off, searched a farmhouse on the American side of the border. Inside they found an empty safe that concealed the entrance to a wide, well-lit tunnel that ran for nearly a mile under the border – a literal pipeline for drugs trafficking.

Massacre and mutilation

The Tijuana cartel's reputation grew to such a degree that the Drug Enforcement Administration in the US declared it 'one of the most powerful, violent and aggressive drug-trafficking organizations in the world'. Despite the cartel's increasing notoriety, however, the brothers were able to carry on without being arrested for thirteen years. To remain free, they spent an estimated million dollars a week on

The brains and the brawn behind the Tijuana cartel; 'El Min' (left) and 'El Mon' (right)

bribing politicians and policemen. Those who held out, or who were not important enough to need bribing in the first place, were simply killed. The brothers murdered hundreds of their enemies – estimates range between three hundred and over a thousand victims. They killed witnesses, bystanders, policemen, two police chiefs, several federal police commanders, judges and even a Roman Catholic cardinal, Juan Jesus Posadas Ocampo. He was gunned down at the airport in Guadalajara when members of the gang mistook his car for that of a rival drug baron. This extraordinary misjudgement led them to lower their profile for a little while, but otherwise traffic and terror went on unabated.

Ramon, in particular, became a notorious figure around Tijuana, driving around in a red Porsche, sporting a mink jacket and heavy gold jewellery. He started to recruit a new type of gangster to the business. These were the so-called 'narco-juniors', rich kids who became hit men for fun rather than profit. Meanwhile, the brothers' brutality became ever more extreme. In 1998, they murdered the entire population of a small fishing village to set an example. Torture and mutilation became part of their way of working as well. A Tijuana prosecutor named Jose Patino Moreno was kidnapped along with two aides. When their bodies were found, they were unrecognizable. Almost every bone in their

Their skills were a classic mix for Latin American drug barons – a lethal mixture of ingenuity and brutality.

bodies had been broken and their heads had been crushed in a vice. Intimidated by the drug traffickers, local police claimed that the three men had died in 'a lamentable traffic incident'. Years later, two policemen would be convicted of involvement in the killings.

The day of reckoning

Very few drug dealers live to enjoy the fruits of their crimes for very long and the Arellano-Felix brothers were no exception. The flamboyant Ramon was the first to go. He got caught up in a shoot-out with a rival drugs gang in Mazatlan, back in Sinaloa province. After the gun battle the police found three corpses, one of which carried ID in the name of Jorge Lopez. Soon afterwards, the body was removed from the undertakers by people claiming to be relatives of the late Mr Lopez. It was only afterwards that the police examined photos of the dead man and identified him as Ramon.

With Ramon's death, the gang's aura of invincibility was shattered. Soon afterwards, Benjamin Arellano-Felix was arrested at a house in the town of Puebla, his bags packed and ready for flight. However, the younger brothers remain at large, and the rise of other drug lords like them has ensured that the multi-million dollar drug-trafficking industry has been barely affected by the fate of the Arellano-Felix brothers.

The ignoble end of one of Mexico's most notorious drug trafficers – Ramon Arellano-Felix lies dead on a curb in Sinaloa province

George Jung

The story of George Jung is a fascinating one. It is the story of how the hippy idealism of the 1960s, based on love, peace and cannabis, slowly developed into a violent culture based on greed, guns and cocaine. The man in the middle of it all was George Jung, who became almost single-handedly responsible for flooding the United States with cocaine in the 1970s. Along the way, Jung lost his ideals, his family and his freedom, and today serves out his sentence in a prison cell.

George Jung grew up in the 1960s in Massachusetts. His father was an honest, hard-working man; his mother a dissatisfied woman, who constantly berated her husband for not earning enough money. The young George left home with a burning desire, above all else, to be rich – an aim he soon achieved. He began by selling marijuana to students in the northeast, before realizing the financial potential of buying it cheap in southern California and Mexico and then transporting it to the east coast of the US, where the street price was much higher. His operation expanded rapidly, until finally one day he was caught. He was tried and sentenced to prison.

'White-collar criminals'

It was in prison that Jung met the men who were later to become his partners in the cocaine trade. At the time, cocaine was a little-known drug in the US, and was hardly used at all. However, from his cell mate, an English-speaking Colombian named Carlos Lehder, Jung learned that cocaine was available cheaply in Colombia and could fetch a very high price in the US. Together, the pair devised a plan for smuggling cocaine from South America into the US. In pursuit of this aim, they met with a number of other prisoners – 'white-collar criminals' as Jung called them – ranging from lawyers and bankers to Indian tribesmen. From a drug smuggler, they learned all they could about navigation, and from a banker, they found out about money laundering.

Once they were released from prison, Lehder and Jung used their new contacts to build up a massive cocaine-trafficking operation. They and the members of their cartel, the Medellin cartel, became responsible for introducing an astonishing eighty-five per cent of the entire amount of cocaine smuggled into the US from the late 1970s to the early 1980s.

Addicted to fear

By this point, Jung was living a life of luxury, having amassed over a hundred million dollars. His money, and his glamorous lifestyle, attracted many female admirers. He met and married a beautiful woman named Mirtha, and the couple had a baby daughter. On a financial and social level, Jung had achieved more than he could ever have hoped for. However, in the process, he had completely lost control of his life. He was addicted to cocaine. He was also addicted, as he later put it, to 'fear': the constant fear of getting caught provided an adrenaline rush that he could not do without, even though he knew that his illegal activities were a threat to his family.

Jung was also fearful about the company he was keeping: by now, he was surrounded by violent criminals such as Pablo Escobar, who supplied the cocaine from Colombia. Escobar not only carried guns but thought nothing of using them; in fact, he once went outside to execute a man during dinner, mentioning to Jung that the man had 'betrayed' him. He then continued his

George Jung went from being a small time pot dealer in California to amassing a million dollar fortune from the cocaine industry. His story was made into the film Blow, *starring Johnny Depp (left)*

dinner. It was incidents like these that made Jung realize that the hippy ideals of love and peace he had started out with had long since vanished, and in their place was a terrifying, evil world of greed, paranoia and violence.

The final collapse

As the cocaine operation became bigger, the risks also grew. Eventually, Jung was arrested. He managed to escape, but was then caught again. His wife left him, taking their baby daughter with her, and he ended up serving a long prison sentence. Everything that he had built up collapsed. Jung had never been a violent man, and was known for his kindness and straight dealing, yet he had allowed himself to become part of a world that had absolutely no moral scruples whatsoever.

Jung's story was later told in a movie, *Blow*. Unusually, the film tried to avoid the stereotype of drug dealers as sleazy lowlifes, and instead portrayed the main characters as dynamic, intelligent men trying to make a success of their lives but eventually succumbing, through greed, to violence and corruption. Like many of his contemporaries, Jung started out with the idea that the government and corporate America were so corrupt that the laws of the land meant nothing; and that drugs such as cannabis and cocaine could be a liberating force for an alternative lifestyle. Yet, through dealing drugs on such a massive scale, and making a personal fortune, Jung fell prey to exactly the same kind of corruption that he pointed to in the establishment. In the process, he introduced new generations into one of the most widely used, destructive and addictive drugs in the United States today: cocaine.

The young George left home with a burning desire, above all else, to be rich – an aim he soon achieved.

Howard Marks

Howard Marks is one of the most audacious drug traffickers of all time. An intelligent, charming man, he managed to import huge amounts of cannabis into the US and Britain, and to elude the authorities while doing so for over twenty years. However, his luck came to an end when Craig Lovato, an agent of the US Drug Enforcement Administration, took it upon himself to bring the elusive Marks to justice. After a long chase, he was finally caught and arrested, and was convicted of drug smuggling. He received a 25-year sentence but was released in 1995 after serving only seven years. Since then, Marks has become a celebrity, writing books about his life and appearing on stage to talk about his adventures. In recent years, he has become a figurehead for pro-cannabis campaigners seeking to legalize the drug.

A charmed life

Marks was born in Britain in 1945, in Port Talbot, Wales, an industrial town dominated by a huge steelworks. In later years, he liked to represent himself as an illiterate miner's son who walked barefoot to school and whose parents kept coal in the bath, but in actual fact his background was fairly comfortable. Howard did well at school, and went on to study at Balliol College, Oxford, arriving there at a time when the 1960s counter-culture was in full swing. He took to supplying cannabis for his friends to enjoy at parties; he attests, however, that he always steered clear of hard drugs such as heroin, especially after a fellow student, Joshua Macmillan (the grandson of the British prime minister), died after an overdose.

On leaving Oxford, Marks began to smuggle drugs, using his sharp wits to come up with clever schemes to evade the authorities. He loved the life, travelling to exotic places and continuing, everywhere he went, to be the life and soul of the party. He began to make a lot of money selling drugs, covering his tracks by opening a boutique in Oxford so that he could pretend his income came from selling clothes. Although he was known by police to be smuggling cannabis, they were unable to catch him; he was too smart for them, and gained the reputation of being 'untouchable'.

Although he was known by police to be smuggling cannabis, they were unable to catch him; he was too smart for them, and gained the reputation of being 'untouchable'.

Howard Marks – 'chilled' even when in hot water

However, by the 1970s, Marks was beginning to get into trouble. He was shipping tons of cocaine across many miles and continents, using a number of different names and money-laundering businesses to evade detection. When he was finally charged with smuggling cannabis, he managed to skip bail and go on the run. However, this did not prevent him from enjoying himself: occasionally, he would show up at parties in New York or London and then, mysteriously, disappear.

The long arm of the law

Marks' next audacious scam landed him in even more trouble. He was accused of shipping fifteen tons of Colombian marijuana into Britain – an enormous, unprecedented amount. However, to everyone's astonishment, at his trial he somehow managed to get off. Marks' criminal activities continued; although during the 1980s he was, on the face of it, living quietly in Spain with his family, he was in fact masterminding cannabis smuggling all over the world. At this time, he is thought to have had about forty-three aliases, twenty-five businesses and ninety phone lines.

Marks continued to outwit the authorities until US drug enforcement agent Craig Lovato decided that enough was enough. Lovato doggedly set out to gather evidence against him, tapping Marks' phone lines and breaking his coded messages to his associates. He found out, for example, that 'Your dog is sick' meant 'Your

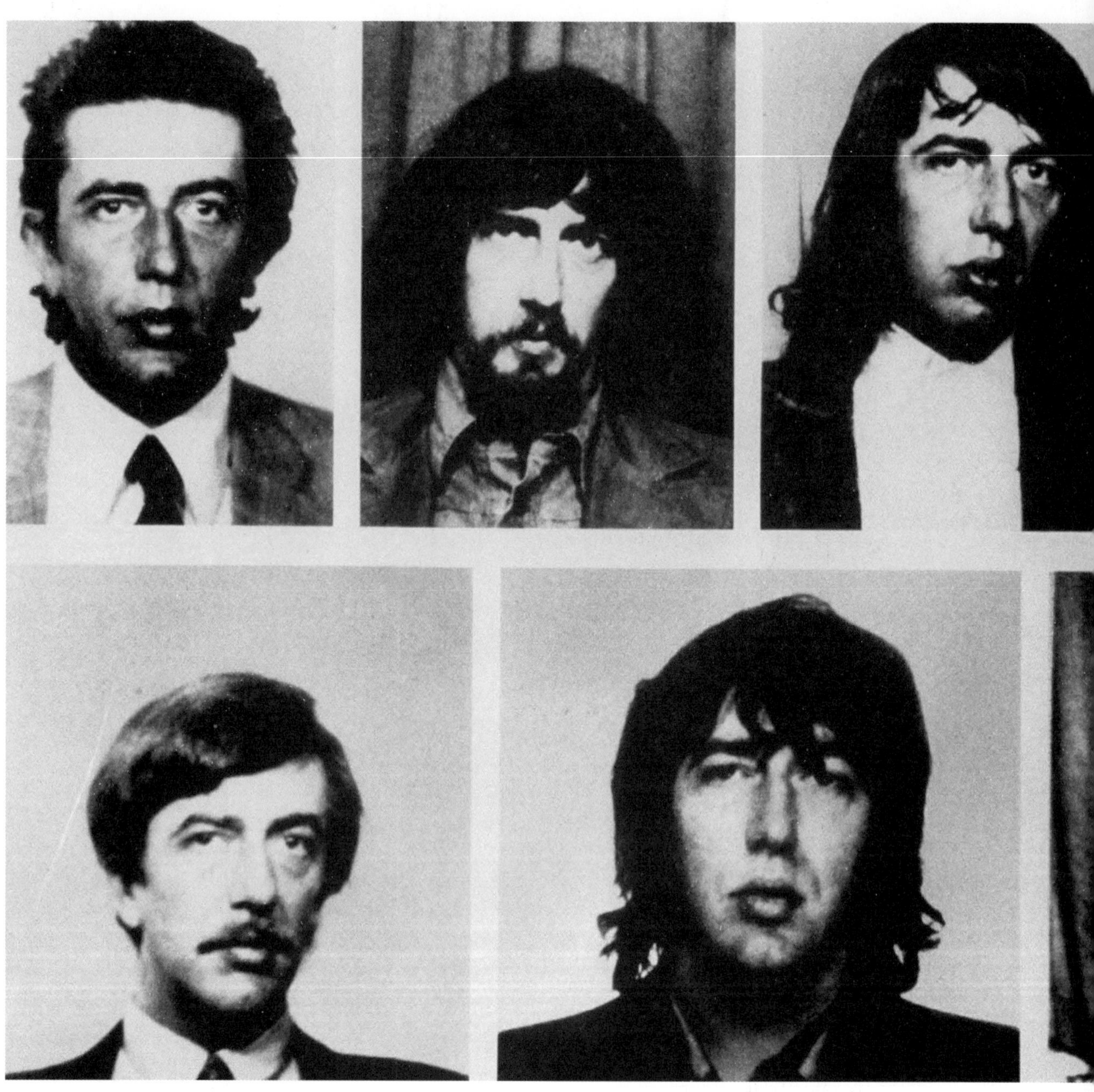

phone is bugged', and that 'champagne' meant 'marijuana'. Lovato kept a detailed record of Marks' drug dealing activities and eventually built up a strong case against him. The final piece fell into place when a business associate and friend of Marks, a rich, decadent aristocrat named Lord Moynihan, informed on him, taping conversations that incriminated Marks and many of his cronies. Marks and twenty-two of his associates were arrested.

Peace, love and cannabis

Marks received a long prison sentence, but only served seven years in jail. He remained unrepentant about his crimes, arguing that cannabis should be legalized, and that he had done nothing wrong. Lovato, for his part, pointed out that Marks had made a great deal of money from his drug-running activities, and that, in the process, he had ruined many of his associates' lives.

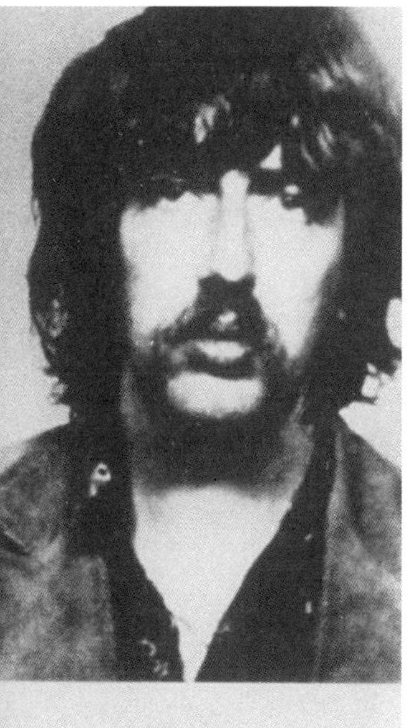

(Left) The many faces and disguises of Howard Marks

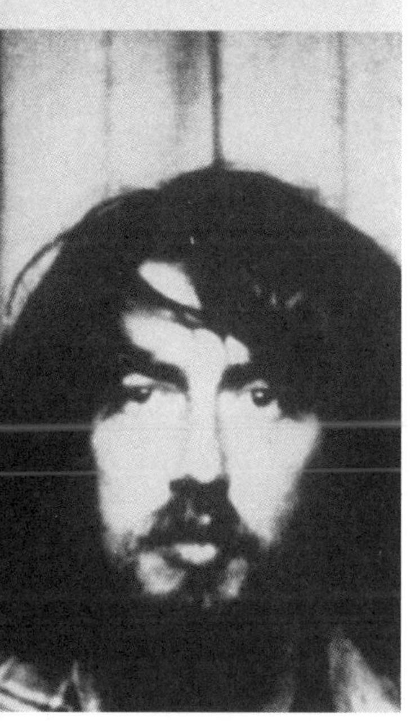

(Right) Still living with the hippy values of peace, love and getting stoned, Howard Marks at Glastonbury Festival

Today, Howard Marks has become something of an icon of the 1960s, and continues to argue his values of peace, love and cannabis to an admiring younger generation, all the while maintaining that his aim was to provide what he saw as a positive, life-enhancing drug to as many people as possible, rather than to amass a fortune for himself and his friends. Whatever his aim, he showed remarkable business acumen, far removed from the hippy image he cultivated.

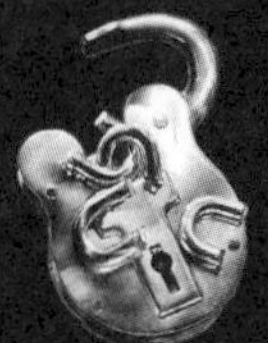

INGENIOUS ESCAPE ARTISTS

The daring deeds of escape artists through the ages, from the eighteenth-century rogue Jack Sheppard to the 1960s vagabond Jacques Mesrine, have always excited the imagination. Sheppard was a thief, much loved by the general public for his ability to escape from the city's most forbidding prisons, including the heavily fortified Newgate Prison; while Mesrine, a good-looking, charismatic jewel thief and kidnapper, outraged Paris by escaping from its maximum security jail, La Sante. Other characters in this section, including Joseph 'Whitey' Riordan, also made their name by outwitting the authorities: Riordan escaped from New York's legendary Sing Sing in 1941, hiding as a fugitive before being found and re-arrested.

The tale of Papillon, perhaps the most notorious of all escape artists, is also told here. Henri Charriere, known as 'Papillon' because of the butterfly tattoo on his chest, achieved lasting fame when he wrote his fascinating life story of escape from some of France's most horrifying penal colonies. What binds these individuals together is an extraordinary level of daring and courage, and an ability to survive all kinds of difficulties. They are also marked by a need to pit themselves against the constraints of the society around them: Charriere settled in a remote village, but within a short time, he felt the urge to return to his former life of escape and capture, leaving the peace and quiet of domestic life behind him.

Jacques Mesrine

Jacques Mesrine was an infamous French bank robber and kidnapper who became known for his daring prison escapes. During the 1960s and 1970s he became popular in France as a romantic 'Robin Hood' figure, who would rob the rich and, allegedly, give to the poor. He was also admired by the public for his ability to outwit the French police force, who were unable for many years to capture him, and eventually named him 'Public Enemy Number One'. The police finally caught up with him on 2 November 1979, and shot him to death.

Mesrine was born into a middle-class family in Clichy, France, in 1936. As a child, he got into trouble at school for his violent behaviour, and was expelled twice. As a young man, he served in Algeria, and then returned to France, where he embarked on a career of crime. A good-looking man, he charmed those around him - sometimes even those he was robbing. However, his courteous exterior belied his true nature, which was that of a ruthless criminal who would stop at nothing to get what he wanted.

A love of publicity

Mesrine liked to live well, enjoying good food and wine at the best restaurants in France. He was extremely attractive to women, and had a succession of beautiful girlfriends, who sometimes accompanied him on his bank robbing sprees. He also dressed well, and often made his raids attired in the height of fashion. All this, of course, together with his love of publicity and his talent for sensational escapades, made him a tremendously popular figure in the national press.

Mesrine's first arrest took place in 1962, when he attempted to rob a bank with three accomplices. He served a sentence in prison and was released the following year. After a short stint working for a design company, he resumed his criminal activities in Spain, and was arrested but set free after only six months. He then opened a restaurant in the Canary Islands, but left to pursue a life of crime once more, first robbing a hotel in Chamonix, France, and then attempting a kidnap in Canada.

Together with his girlfriend, Jeanne Schneider, Mesrine planned to kidnap a Canadian grocery and textile millionaire named Georges Deslauriers. Deslauriers had employed Mesrine and Schneider as domestic servants and then sacked them. The kidnap failed, and Mesrine and Schneider were sentenced to ten years in prison for the attempt. However, they managed to escape in style, capturing a prison warder, stealing his keys, locking him in a cell and fleeing to live in the woods.

He decided to return to the prison and help all of the remaining inmates of the prison to escape.

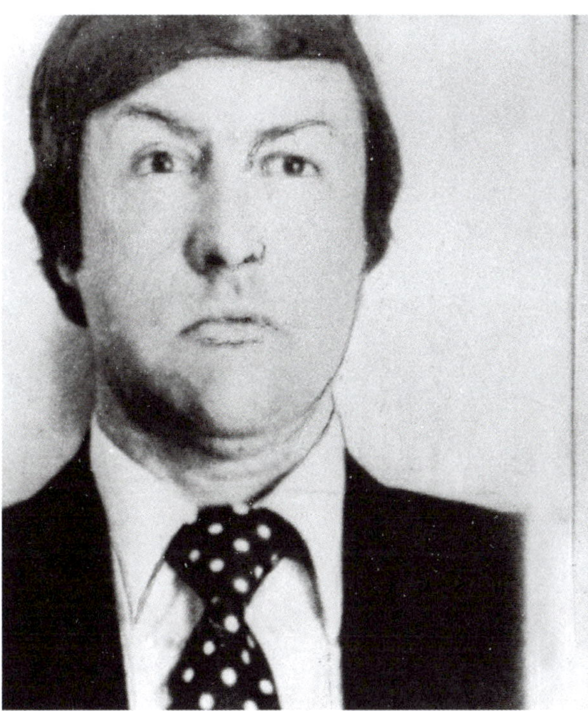

The changing faces of Jaques Mesrine. He seemed to delight in coming up with different disguises with which to outwit the police

Sensational escapes

Mesrine was soon recaptured, and this time sent to the high-security Saint Vincent de Paul prison outside Montreal. Before long, he had led five inmates in a daring escape that involved using a pair of pliers stolen from a workshop to cut through several fences. After managing this extraordinary feat, the group then flagged down cars on the highway, and got clean away.

Mesrine's next move was audacious in the extreme: he decided to return to the prison and help the remaining inmates of the prison to escape. He robbed a number of banks to raise the money he needed, and then went back, armed with shotguns and wire cutters. However, the complicated plan failed and Mesrine had to make a quick getaway. He was on the run once more.

Courtroom drama

With his accomplice Jean-Paul Mercier, Mesrine fled to Venezuela. However, before long he was back in France, robbing banks again. In 1973, he was caught and tried. During his trial in court, he caused a sensation by managing to take a judge hostage. An accomplice had hidden a gun for him in one of the toilets of the court, which he stuffed into his belt and pulled out as his charges were being read. Holding on to the judge and using him as a human shield, he ran under a hail of bullets from police, jumped into a getaway car and sped away. He was arrested several months later and imprisoned once more.

Mesrine's next sensational exploit was to escape from his maximum security jail at La Sante de Paris. Using a secret stash of guns, Mesrine and two other prisoners held up guards, stole their uniforms and locked them in the cells. They then commandeered some ladders and climbed over the prison walls, using ropes and grappling irons. They became the first prisoners ever to escape from La Sante. The incident infuriated the French authorities, who were completely humiliated by Mesrine's disappearance from their top-security prison.

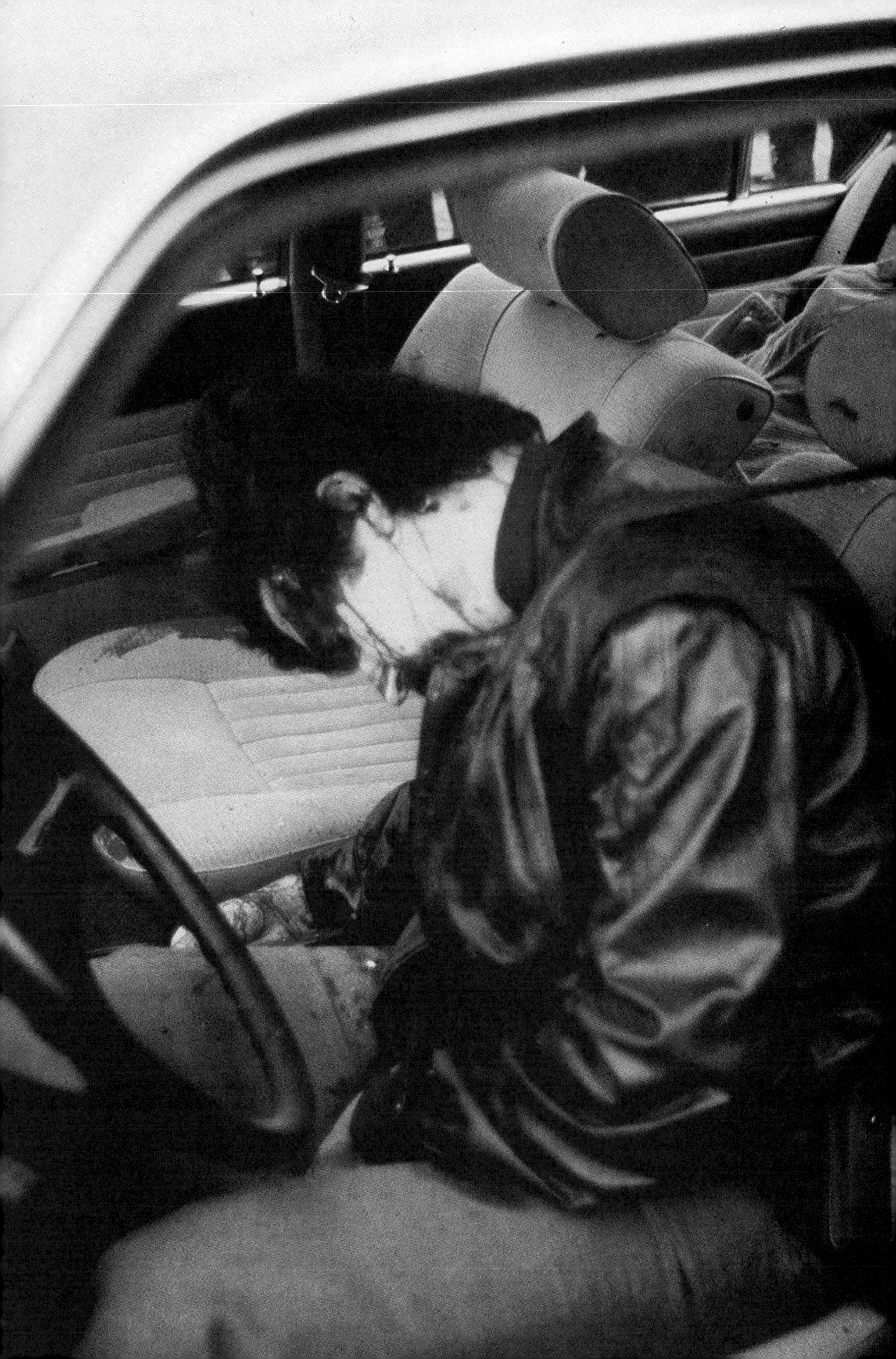

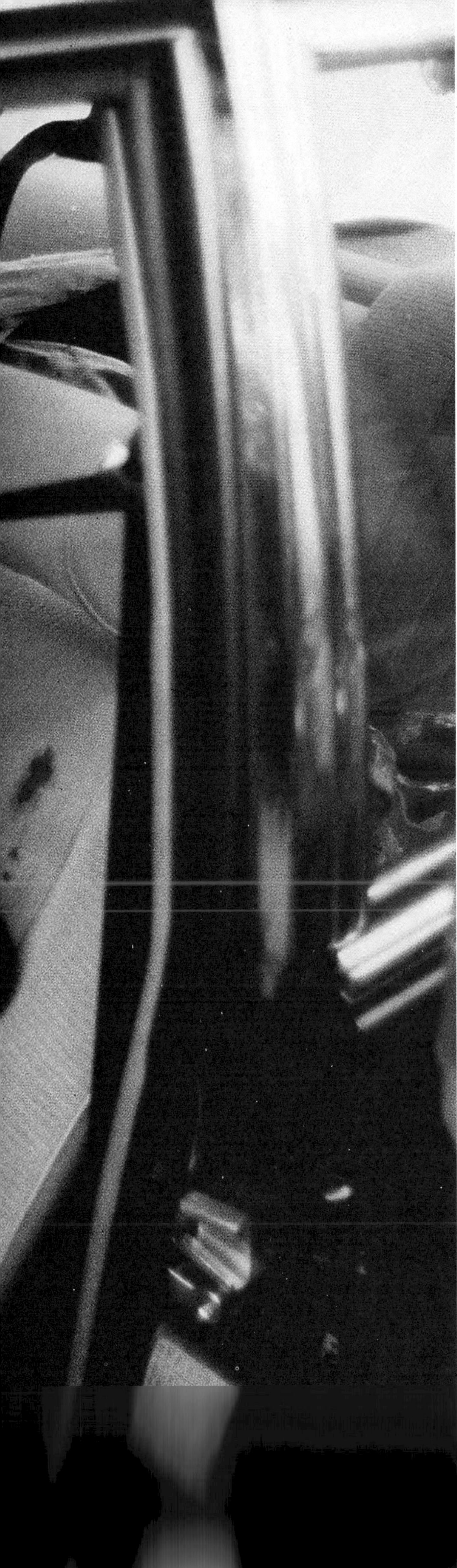

Mesrine now became the most wanted man in the country.

The final showdown

Free once more, Mesrine continued his criminal career, becoming ever more daring – and ruthless. He used a variety of disguises to evade police during his exploits, including wigs, which he sometimes wore one on top of the other for quick changes. He kidnapped rich individuals, robbed banks and jewellery shops, and smuggled arms. He boasted that he had killed over thirty victims in the process of committing his crimes, although this figure has never been verified. Despite this, sections of the French press continued to view him as a romantic figure, painting him as a kind of Robin Hood, a thorn in the side of authority. Mesrine, too, evidently saw himself as a folk hero, and often attempted in interviews to convince journalists that his crimes were motivated by radical political ideas rather than by self-interest. The fact that he had boasted about cold-bloodedly murdering scores of victims, and that he obviously spent more money than he ever gave away, did not stop the tabloid press from seeing him as something of a hero – perhaps because his escapades made the French authorities look so foolish and inept.

As Mesrine's criminal activities continued, the French government became more and more embarrassed by him, and ordered police departments to intensify their efforts to catch him. On 2 November 1979, police found out where he was living and ambushed his car, surrounding it as he waited at traffic lights in the street. They shot nineteen rounds of bullets through his windscreen, killing him instantly.

The legend ends: Mesrine was gunned down at close range while waiting at traffic lights

Papillon

Henri Charriere was a small-time Parisian crook who achieved lasting fame when he wrote his life story, entitled *Papillon.* The book told of the many thrilling adventures that befell this highly intelligent, resourceful criminal as he planned escapes from various prisons in South America, where he was sent after being convicted of murder in 1931. Charriere's escapes were carefully planned, but he also learned to take opportunities when they arose, using the skills he had learned as a thief on the streets of his native city. The title of the autobiography, French for 'butterfly', was Charriere's nickname which derived from a tattoo of a butterfly that he had on his chest.

Charriere grew up in Paris and, as a young man, began a criminal career as a thief and safe-breaker. He managed for the most part to evade the law until, in 1931, he was accused of murdering a pimp named Roland le Petit. He maintained that he had been framed for the murder, but no one believed him. When the case came to trial, he was found guilty and sentenced to a term of life imprisonment with hard labour. He was ordered to serve out his sentence at a penal colony in French Guiana, which was infamous at the time for its brutality and tough living conditions.

Prison camp ordeal

In the book, Charriere described in detail the horrific conditions for prisoners in the penal colony of French Guiana at that period. He also made it clear that, although he was no angel, and had for many years made his living as a thief, he was innocent of the crime of murder that he had been convicted of. His abiding sense of outrage that he had become the victim of a miscarriage of justice carries the reader's sympathies; it also helps to explain the iron determination that Charriere showed throughout his long career as an escape artist, making every effort to break out of his confinement at every opportunity, whatever the cost.

Once at the penal colony, Papillon effected the first of many bids for freedom. He escaped from hospital on the mainland in the company of two other prisoners, and made his way to Riohacha, Colombia. He sailed along the coast, via Trinidad and Curacao, for hundreds of miles in an open boat. After this gruelling ordeal, he finally reached Colombia, only to be caught there and imprisoned once again.

Escape and capture

Undaunted, Charriere escaped and went on the run again, this time to Guajira, where he lived in a native village and took two wives as his consorts. This episode in his eventful life was a relatively peaceful one, in which he lived in peace and harmony with his wives, Lali and Zoraima. Their relaxed attitude towards sex pleased him greatly, differing entirely as it did from the mores of the French women he had known. Both of his wives eventually became pregnant by him. However, although he could probably have carried on living in the village for the rest of his life, working and raising his children in obscurity, his lust for adventure caused him to move on. When he did so, he was once again captured and imprisoned, this time at Santa Marta.

Charriere was then moved to Barranquilla, where he made various audacious attempts to escape, but these all failed. In 1934, he was sent

The lined face of an experienced escape artist – Charriere's adventures made for a lively lifestyle

back to French Guiana, where he was punished for his escape attempts by being put into solitary confinement on the island of St Joseph. After two years of a miserably lonely existence, he was sent to another island, Royale, where he again attempted to escape. However, on this occasion his attempt was foiled by an informer, whom he murdered.

Once again, Charriere was punished; and once again, he continued to make his escape attempts from wherever he was imprisoned. It seemed that nothing would deter him. His next ruse was to pretend to be mad, so that he was sent to the mental hospital on the island of St Joseph. He attempted to escape from the hospital, but was caught and transferred to Devil's Island.

Freedom at last

As its name suggests, Devil's Island was a hellish place, rife with disease, where prisoners lived under a brutal regime in fear of their lives. Legend had it that no prisoner had ever escaped from the island – until Papillon came along, that is. Not surprisingly, soon after arriving, Charriere made his bid for freedom, throwing himself into the shark-infested sea surrounding the island with only a makeshift raft of coconut sacking to keep him afloat in the water. Against all odds, he succeeded in reaching the mainland, and once there travelled on to Georgetown. In company with five other fugitives, he managed to get to Venezuela, but once there, was taken prisoner at El Dorado.

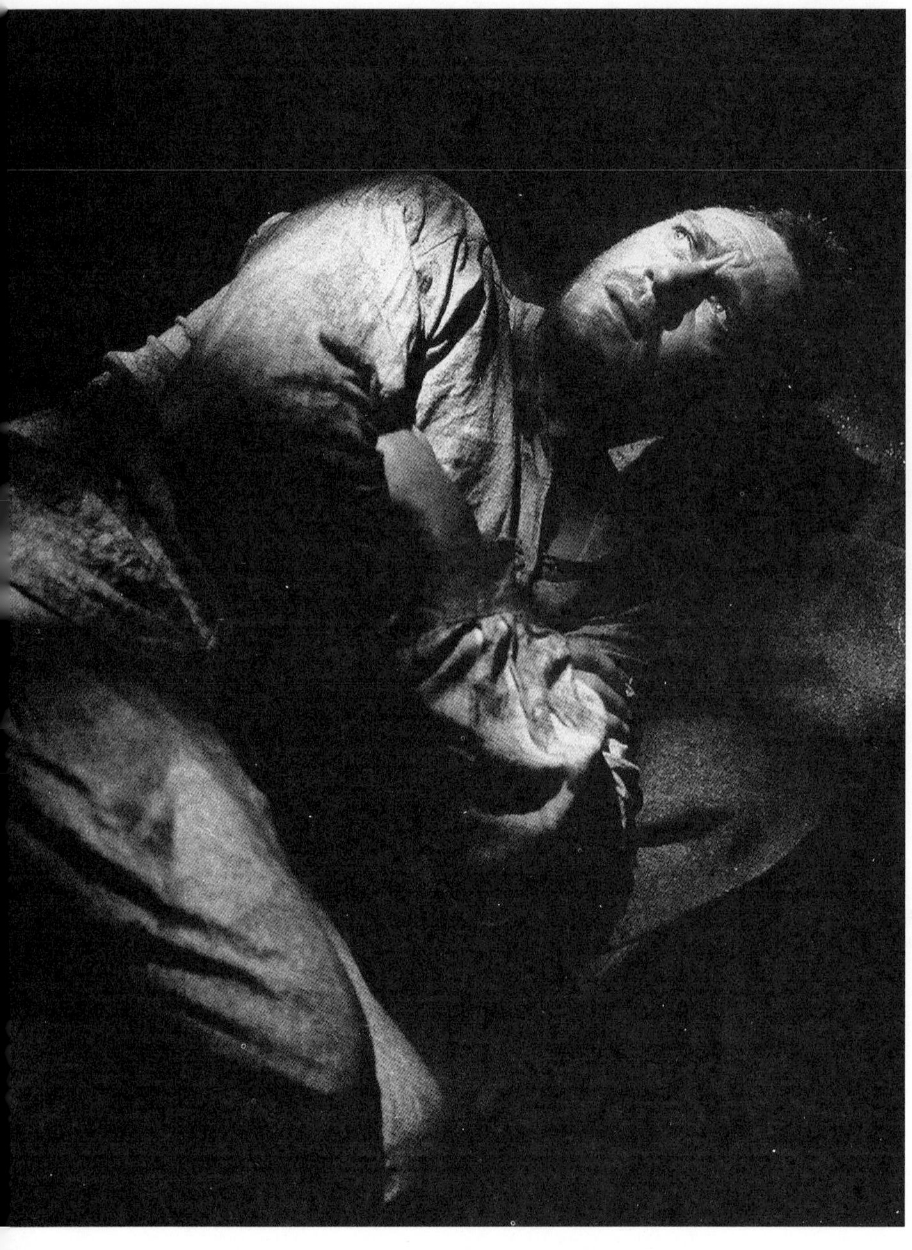

Legend had it that no prisoner had ever escaped from the island – until Papillon came along.

Charriere's book Papillon *was made into a film of the same name, which starred Steve McQueen*

Charriere was finally given his freedom in 1945. He settled in Venezuela, and opened a restaurant in Caracas where he entertained diners with stories of his many adventures on the run from the law. He died in 1973 at the age of sixty-six.

Today, some critics question Charriere's innocence, wondering whether he was in actual fact the unfortunate victim of a miscarriage of justice that he made himself out to be. Others claim that he exaggerated his story, and that parts of it cannot be true. Another criticism levelled at him is that his casual attitude to his two native wives (whom he impregnated and then left), not to mention his disregard for his own family back home in France, showed him to be a philanderer. However, despite these criticisms, his autobiography continues to be read by hundreds of new readers every year, and is still enjoyed as an inspiring testament to the human spirit of endurance, determination, and the search for justice.

Joseph 'Whitey' Riordan

A grim place, the interior of Sing Sing no doubt spurred on Whitey Riordan's endeavours to escape

Joseph Riordan, nicknamed 'Whitey', was one of the few prisoners to escape from the legendary Sing Sing, New York's maximum security prison. He came up with a master plan to make the perfect escape, and succccdcd in breaking out of the jail. His daring breakout, along with two other prisoners, took place on 13 April 1941, and went down in history as the most serious breach of security ever to occur at the prison.

Riordan and his two accomplices, John

'Patch' Waters and Charles McGale, were all prisoners who had been convicted of armed robbery and sent to Sing Sing to serve out their sentences. They met when they were being held in the prison hospital, and between them hatched an audacious escape plan. They contacted outside accomplices, who smuggled guns into them while they were in the hospital. Armed with the guns, they chose a quiet moment to launch their attempt, when few guards were on duty.

The bid for freedom

At 2.30 am they pulled out their guns and began their bid for freedom. A prison guard, John Hartye, was making his rounds of the wards at this time; when he tried to stop them, they shot him in the back. This incident caused another inmate, McGowan Miller, who was ill in the hospital, to suffer a serious heart attack. The shock was so severe that he died instantly.

Leaving this trail of devastation behind them, the three prisoners then made their way down into the prison basement. There they found another guard, pulled their guns on him, and forced him at gunpoint to lead them out of the prison. The group made their way through a tunnel they knew about that led out into the street outside the prison. They had previously arranged, with outside accomplices, for a getaway car to meet them there and it was waiting for them.

As the escapees ran towards the waiting car, two police officers, William Nelson and James Fagan, just happened to be walking up the street. Seeing the prisoners, they became suspicious, and stopped them. Riordan lost his head and drew out his gun. He began to shoot wildly, at which point Waters and McGale also pulled out their revolvers and joined in. The policemen responded by opening fire as well, and soon a street gunfight was raging, with bullets ricocheting all around. During the battle, one of the prisoners, Waters, was shot dead with two bullets in the head; one of the policemen, Fagan, was also wounded by a shot to the head. The police officer was rushed to hospital, but it was too late to save him: he was pronounced dead on arrival.

Brought to justice

Riordan and McGale fled the scene, and went down to the river side. There, they found a fisherman, Charles Rohr, to carry them across the Hudson river in his boat. Once on the other side, they disappeared into the woods and hid, but not for long. They were eventually found by police, using a pack of bloodhounds to sniff them out. The pair were arrested, as were the accomplices who had supplied the prisoners with guns.

When the case came to trial, Riordan mounted a defence claiming that police officers had beaten him until he made a confession. He recounted how he and McGale had been kicked, punched and knocked to the ground hundreds of times when in custody. He also alleged that they had been strung up and tortured. However, the judge and jury were not sympathetic, and both men received the death sentence. Their accomplices were given life sentences.

In a final irony, Riordan was executed on 11 June 1942; his birthday.

They were eventually found by police, using a pack of bloodhounds to sniff them out.

Jack Sheppard

Newgate Prison, one hundred years on, was still just as unprepossessing as it was in Sheppard's day

Jack Sheppard was an eighteenth-century thief who achieved notoriety because of his amazing ability to escape the long arm of the law. Arrested and imprisoned several times, he managed several dramatic escapes from some of the harshest prisons in England, using a combination of meticulous planning, sharp-witted resourcefulness and street savvy. After his death, he went down in history as one of the great characters of British crime history, and was immortalised in poems, books, plays and films.

John Sheppard was born in Spitalfields, London, in 1702. He was the son of a carpenter, but while he was a boy his father died, and the family became poverty-stricken. His mother found him an apprenticeship in his late father's trade. While he was working, he began to mix with London low life, frequenting a London pub called the Black Lion in Drury Lane. Here he consorted with prostitutes and, at their suggestion, began to supplement his meagre earnings by stealing goods from the houses where he was working. He then, under the influence of a woman named Maggot, progressed to breaking and entering.

A life of debauchery

Before long, Jack fell out with his employers, who disliked the company he was keeping and suspected him of stealing. He was by now leading a wild, debauched life in the company of villains, so he gave up his apprenticeship entirely and began thieving full time. He achieved notoriety when, on a visit to one of his prostitute friends in prison, a woman named Edgworth Bess, he had a violent altercation with a guard, knocked him down, and carried the lady

He had a violent altercation with a guard, knocked him down, and carried the lady out of the prison. This exploit, not surprisingly, made him extremely popular with the prostitutes of London.

out of the prison. This exploit made him popular with the prostitutes of London, and also endeared him to the British public generally.

Jack then went into partnership with his brother Thomas, and together the brothers and Edgworth Bess committed a series of robberies in London. This went on until one of his drinking cronies – hoping to gain a reward – told the police of his whereabouts. Sheppard was arrested and sent to St Giles' Prison.

Prison escapes

At St Giles', Sheppard made his first escape by sawing through the wooden ceiling of his cell. Once outside, he met up with Edgworth Bess again and committed several more offences, until he was rearrested and this time, sent to the infamous Newgate Prison, supposedly one of the most secure prisons in Britain. He escaped from Newgate three times during that year. On the first occasion, he cut a hole in his cell wall and used his bed sheets to climb down to the street. On the second, he cut a metal spike out of a window. After that, he was locked up in a strong room called the 'castle', from where he made his third escape.

In the castle, Sheppard was put in handcuffs and leg irons which were chained to the floor. His jailors were doing their best to ensure he had no means of escape. He was allowed visitors – and he had many, his fame having spread far and wide – but they were very carefully monitored so that they could not pass him items such as knives, chisels, and so on. However, Sheppard managed to find a small nail in the room, and somehow unlocked the padlock that connected the chain to the staple on the floor. He was able to take off his handcuffs and fetters, and then found a large iron bar in the chimney, which he took with him. To leave the prison he then had to pick the locks of several bolted doors, wrench off bars and break down walls with the iron bar he had got from the chimney. He used some bedclothes to swing up to the roof of a house nearby the prison, and made his escape over the rooftops of the city.

Sentenced to be hanged

After two weeks, Sheppard was arrested again. He was once again sent to Newgate, and this time was sentenced to be hanged on the gallows. Still undeterred, he planned another escape. One of his visitors had given him a penknife, which he was apparently going to use to cut the ropes binding his body as he was led to the gallows. His plan had been to jump into the crowd, which he knew would be friendly and help him to escape. However, before he set off for his final journey, a prison warder found the penknife.

As he went through the streets of London, he received a hero's welcome. He was then hanged at Tyburn. He was only twenty-three years old. Afterwards his body was cut down and taken by friends to a pub in Long Acre. In the evening, the body was buried at the church of St Martin's-in-the-Fields.

Sheppard's exploits were remembered long after his death. In the eighteenth century, he became the model for the character of Macheath in *The Beggar's Opera*. In the nineteenth century, he was immortalised in plays and a novel, while in the twentieth, he appears in Brecht and Weill's *The Threepenny Opera*.

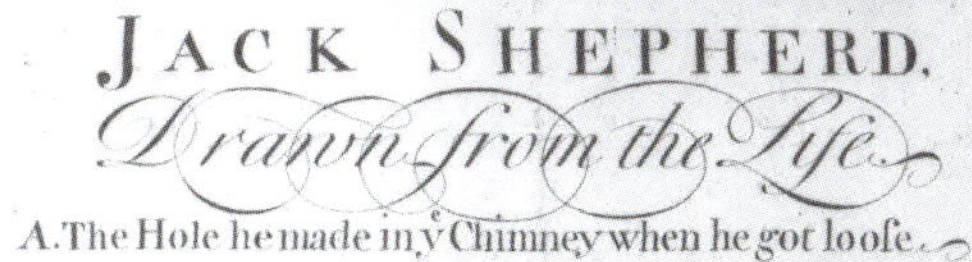

Jack Sheppard caught the imagination – although not the accuracy (of his name's spelling) – of the popular press as can be seen by both these pictures

UNFLAPPABLE FRAUDSTERS

In a sense, fraudsters are the most psychologically straightforward of the criminal masterminds. Here are people who act out of greed and self-interest but who, for the most part, are not violent people. Their escapades show a degree of courage, skill and sheer audacity that is out of the ordinary. They are often colourful, larger-than-life characters whose devil-may-care attitude to life impresses and excites us. For the most part, their crimes are financial: their victims are often large corporations or rich individuals rather than ordinary people. However, although on the surface these criminals appear to act from rational, relatively 'normal' motives, close examination of their stories often reveals the reverse to be the case.

Many of them seem to have a compulsion to repeat the same tricks until they get caught. Take, for example, Count Victor Lustig, who in the early years of the twentieth century succeeded in pulling off an amazing scam, which was to pose as a government official and 'sell' the Eiffel Tower to a group of dealers in scrap metal. Not content with his initial success, Lustig repeated the con, and the second time was caught. In the same way, Frank Abagnale Jr, whose story amazed readers when it was published, began by posing as an airline pilot in the 1960s, and then went on to become a bogus doctor, lawyer and university lecturer, before returning to his first role again – and getting arrested. It seems that for the fraudsters, from the eighteenth-century charlatan Jonathan Wild to the twentieth-century master art forger Han van Meegeren, seeing how far one can push one's luck is the major motivation in the game of crime.

Frank Abagnale Jr

Frank Abagnale Jr is one of the most outrageous con men of all time. During his career of crime, he impersonated a Pan Am pilot and flew around the world, enjoying the high life, before posing as a paediatrician and finding a senior job in a Georgia hospital. As if that were not enough, he then found employment as a bogus lawyer in the office of the state attorney general, before going on to claim he had a degree in sociology and becoming a university lecturer. Yet, amazingly, Abagnale was in fact a high-school dropout with no qualifications whatsoever to his name; and even more unbelievably, all this took place before he was twenty-one years of age. However, he did end up with a high degree of knowledge in one particular field: today, he is an expert on counterfeiting.

Frank Abagnale Jr was born in 1948. His early family life was uncomplicated, but when he was a teenager, his parents divorced. He took to spending money on his father's credit cards, running up huge bills as he tried to impress young women with his lavish lifestyle. His father, who ran a stationery store, was kind and patient with his son but nevertheless soon faced financial ruin. At this point, Abagnale ran away from home.

Looking more like someone's uncle than a highly successful fraudster, Abagnale helped the US authorities with cases of fraud whilst he was in prison

'The Skywayman'

At the age of sixteen, Abagnale found himself in New York City, looking for a job. Luckily for him, he looked older than he really was – in fact, his hair was already beginning to turn grey – and so found it easy to pretend that he was about ten years older than his actual age. This, of course, involved altering his driving licence. After that, he realized the potential of counterfeiting, and never looked back.

His first target was his bank account. He changed numbers on deposit slips in the bank, so that money went into his account every time a customer made a deposit at the bank. He also wrote hundreds of bad cheques himself and overdrew massively on his account. In this way, he made and spent thousands of dollars. His next move was to impersonate a Pan Am pilot using a uniform he acquired by phoning an outfitter's, telling them that he had lost his uniform, and charging the account to a fictitious employee of the company. He got a special pass by contacting the company who made the passes for Pan Am and telling them he needed a sample. He added his own logo to the pass by taking one from a model aeroplane kit. He then turned up at airports and asked for a free ride on TWA aeroplanes, having found out through extensive study of the aviation industry about a practice known as 'deadheading', in which airlines helped each other out by carrying pilots from other companies in available remaining seats. Each time he flew, his expenses would be billed to Pan Am. When his ruse was discovered, he became known as 'The Skywayman'.

The fake medic

During the 1960s, when Abagnale was masquerading as a pilot, the aviation industry was held in high esteem. With his uniform and his passes (which even included a pilot's licence that he had forged), Abagnale found that he was able to cash cheques anywhere, and that people immediately trusted and respected him. He also became very popular with women, most of them air hostesses a good deal older than himself. However, despite the thousands of dollars he amassed, and the exciting life of travel and adventure that he was leading, he later admitted to being quite lonely at this point, since he was always on the run from the police and could confide in no one.

He decided to change tack, and settled for a while in Georgia, where he pretended to be a doctor in order to rent an apartment more easily. He soon became acquainted with a 'fellow' doctor, who asked him to help out temporarily at his hospital. Amazingly enough, given the fact that he did not even have a high-school diploma, let alone a qualification in medicine, nobody noticed Abagnale's lack of knowledge. He often covered his ignorance by joking with staff, who warmed to his jovial manner, and accepted his authority completely.

Changing identity - again

Realizing that his cover would soon be blown, and that he was in danger of causing his patients real damage, Abagnale moved on, this time to Louisiana. He forged documents to show that he was a lawyer, and even passed exams. He enjoyed his new job, before realizing that it was only a matter of time before his deception was

As Abagnale was serving out his sentence, the US government approached him and asked him to help them solve some of their many fraud cases.

Perhaps crime can pay? Frank Abagnale Jr with director Steven Spielberg at the premiere of the film made of his life Catch Me If You Can

discovered, so he left and took up a new career – this time as a sociology lecturer. This pattern of change continued until he finally returned to his old role as an airline pilot – this time with a crew of beautiful young 'air hostesses' to assist him. In all, he changed his identity many times, becoming a series of different people with different aliases. He also became extremely adept at forging cheques, and amassed millions of dollars in this way.

It was not long, of course, before Abagnale was being pursued by international law enforcement agencies across the world. He was wanted in all American states and in twenty-six countries worldwide. However, his extraordinary career of deception and fraud finally came to an end when, at the age of twenty-one, he was arrested as he attempted to board an Air France aeroplane. He was tried and convicted in France, and spent several years in prison in Europe before returning to the US, where he was sentenced to a further term of imprisonment.

The model businessman

As Abagnale was serving out his sentence, the US government approached him and asked him to help them solve some of their many fraud cases, by showing them the workings of this kind of crime from the inside. Abagnale agreed, and was duly released. He then set up a company, paid off his debts, married and had a family, and since that time has used his remarkable skills to catch other criminals.

In 1980, Abagnale co-wrote the story of his life, entitled *Catch Me If You Can*. Within weeks it topped the bestseller lists, and was hugely popular around the world. The book later became the basis of a film starring Leonardo diCaprio.

D. B. Cooper

The name D. B. Cooper refers to an aeroplane hijacker who hit the headlines in 1971, first extorting money and then parachuting out of the plane. He was never found, and thus the incident remains a mystery, prompting a great deal of speculation as to who the hijacker was and what became of him.

The hijacker made his appearance on 24 November 1971, on the eve of Thanksgiving. He bought his one-way ticket under the name of Dan Cooper and boarded his plane, a Northwest Orient Airlines Boeing 727, flying from Portland, Oregon, to Seattle, Washington. He was a well-dressed, middle-aged man, and did not attract attention in any way.

Did he survive to spend his ill-gotten gains? A photofit made up from airport staff's descriptions of the mysterious D. B. Cooper

'No funny stuff'

At that period, aeroplane hijackings were relatively common. However, most of them were political in nature, designed to attract attention to an anti-establishment cause. Cooper was unusual in this area in that he was, apparently, a conventional man who appears to have pulled off his stunt for one reason only: money.

Cooper sat at the back of the plane as it took off, and passed a note to the air hostess, Flo Schaffner. In the note, he wrote that he had brought a bomb on board, and wanted two hundred thousand dollars in unmarked bills, four parachutes and 'no funny stuff'. Ms Schaffner was used to male passengers passing her notes asking for a date, so she simply put the note in her pocket. It was only when the plane was taking off that she read it. She immediately told the flight crew about the note, and they radioed the airport for help. Meanwhile, Ms Schaffner went to talk to Cooper, to see if he really did have a bomb. When he opened his briefcase, she saw some red sticks and some wires, which convinced her that he was telling the truth.

Before the plane landed, the FBI sent a message to say that the parachutes and money would be available for the hijacker at the airport. In accordance with the hijacker's demands, the bills would be unmarked – but unbeknown to him, they had all been copied on a Xerox machine, so that the serial numbers could be traced later.

Escape by parachute

Once the plane landed, Cooper let all the passengers off. He then waited for the money and parachutes to be delivered to the plane. It is likely that he asked for four parachutes because he was afraid that if only one was delivered, it would be deliberately faulty. By asking for four, he was confusing the authorities, who may have thought the other parachutes were intended for members of the flight crew, and would therefore ensure that all of them were working properly.

Cooper asked the pilot to fly to Mexico at a low height, with the landing gear and plane flaps down. The pilot told the hijacker that, because the plane was flying low, it would be necessary to stop for refuelling in Reno, Nevada, on the way. Cooper agreed to touch down in Reno. On the flight there, he asked the crew to remain in the cockpit and told the stewardess to close the curtain in the first-class section behind them. The last the crew saw of him was when he was trying to tie something around his waist, most probably the bag of money that he had received.

A while later, the pilot noticed that the warning light to show that a door was open on the plane had come on. He shouted out to ask if there was anything they could do for the hijacker, who responded 'No!'. Cooper then disappeared, apparently by jumping off the back staircase of the plane, which he had forced open.

Vanishing into the blue

Despite the fact that the plane was being followed by air force planes and an FBI helicopter, the hijacker was not seen jumping out. When the plane landed in Reno, it was searched, but all that remained of the hijacker were two parachutes, some cigarette ends, a tie and a tie clip. Cooper had completely vanished.

No one knows to this day whether he survived his parachute jump out of the plane. The plane was flying at almost two hundred miles an hour through a temperature of minus seven degrees Celsius, with a wind chill factor of minus seventy degrees. However, Cooper may have survived this, because he would not have remained in these temperatures for more than about fifteen seconds before landing. Even so, he was not dressed for parachuting through winter conditions, wearing only a suit and an overcoat. When he landed in the snowy forest below without adequate clothing or provisions, he might well have frozen to death overnight.

Although a huge search of the area was made, and two bodies were eventually found (both missing persons, neither of them connected to the case), there was no trace of the hijacker. Many years later, in 1980, some of the twenty-dollar bills that he had taken turned up. They were found on the shore of a river near Vancouver, Washington, by a boy and his family on a picnic. The total amount was over five thousand dollars, and the serial numbers on the bills matched the ones copied by the FBI almost a decade before. The police took in a man named Daniel B. Cooper for questioning, but released him since he appeared to have no connection with the case. (After this episode, the case became known as that of 'D. B. Cooper', even though the hijacker had only given his name as Dan.)

In the end, the finding of the bills did little to solve the mystery. Nobody was any the wiser as to where the hijacker had disappeared to, or what he had done with the rest of the money. To this day, the case of D. B. Cooper remains a riddle.

Nobody was any the wiser as to where the hijacker had disappeared that winter night, or what he had done with the rest of the money.

Martin Frankel

Martin Frankel conducted one of the most far-reaching series of frauds in the history of the US financial world. With no formal qualifications and a string of failed business ventures behind him, he managed to pose as an investment specialist and persuade several skilled, intelligent people to part with their money and involve themselves in his scams. He showed no moral scruples whatsoever, and for many years got away with his crimes. However, his insecurity and paranoia finally got the better of him, and he was eventually brought to justice when his trail of lies was uncovered.

Born in Toledo, Ohio, in 1954, Frankel's father was a well-respected Lucas County judge, Leon Frankel. Martin was the second child of the family. He was a bright pupil at school and did well at his studies, but socially he was a misfit. After leaving high school, he went on to study at the University of Toledo, but dropped out of his course before finishing it. He had developed a crippling fear of taking tests, and was also completely unable to discipline himself to work. It seems that his early success at school had been achieved without trying very hard, and he had later become anxious about any situation in which he had to make an effort, or in which there was a chance of being seen to fail.

After dropping out of college, Frankel began to take an interest in the world of finance. He believed that by researching and playing the securities market, he could earn a great deal of money very quickly – which, fortunatcly, proved to be the case. Unfortunately, however, he did not also take into account that he could also lose it just as quickly, especially if he had gained it under false pretences.

Martin Frankel is helped out of a car on the way to his trial in Hamburg. Having had the potential for a glittering future, his choice to go down the path of criminality was a particularly poor one

Martin Frankel's luxury house in Greenwich, Connecticut – just one of the assets he had to give up when arrested and found guilty of fraud and racketeering

Fear of failure

Frankel took to hanging around brokerage houses, learning as much as he could about the finance business. He took a particular interest in big fraud cases, such as that of Robert Vesco, who had masterminded one of the largest swindles in US history. He met many business people, befriending a couple named John and Sonia Schulte, who owned a securities business affiliated to the New York company of Dominick & Dominick. Frankel impressed the couple with his knowledge of the market and with a scheme that he said could help him predict which stocks would yield a great deal of money in future.

Sonia Schulte persuaded her husband to take Frankel on as a consultant analyst, but it was not long before John Schulte regretted his decision. Frankel was not a good employee. He refused to conform to the company's dress code, turning up for work in jeans rather than a suit and tie. His money-making scheme was also failing to yield any good results. One of the problems was that, although Frankel knew how to analyze the market, he did not actually have the confidence to trade. As with taking tests at school, he feared that he would be seen to fail.

The final straw for Schulte was when Frankel posed as an agent working for the larger affiliated firm of Dominick & Dominick, a move that could have put his boss out of business. Schulte lost patience with his new employee and fired him. However, that was by no means the end of his relationship with Frankel: for, by this time, Frankel had become Sonia's lover.

The Vatican fraud

Now unemployed and living at his parents' house, Frankel set up his own bogus investment business, which he named Winthrop Capital. He advertised in the yellow pages, and gained the trust of several clients, telling all sorts of lies to do so. However, his investments were not sound, and he lost a great deal of money on his clients' behalf. Not deterred, he set up another business, Creative Partners Fund LP. He was joined by Sonia Schulte, who by this time had left her husband. Together, the pair set up another company, Thunor Trust, and began buying failing insurance companies, doing shady deals to fund their ever more lavish lifestyle.

Frankel's next, and most bizarre, scam was to mastermind a fraudulent charity scheme with links to the Vatican. Posing as a wealthy philanthropist, he set up a body called the St Francis of Assisi Foundation, and made several important contacts: with Thomas Bolan, founder of the Conservative Party of New York; and with two well-known New York priests, Peter Jacobs and Emilio Colagiovanni. It was a complicated fraud, involving the buying and selling of insurance companies with funds certified to belong to the Vatican, but the lure for all parties was a simple one: money.

Sadomasochistic orgies

By 1998, Frankel's assets were over four million dollars. He and Sonia moved to a large mansion in Greenwich, Connecticut, together with Sonia's two daughters. However, the new family home was not a happy one. Frankel began to show a greedy sexual appetite and a cruel streak, surrounding himself with young women and hosting sadomasochistic orgies in the house. Sonia soon left with her daughters. In 1997, one of the young women living in the house, who had apparently been rejected by Frankel, hanged herself there.

By 1999, Frankel's many nefarious dealings were finally attracting the attention of the authorities. His companies were put under state supervision, and it seemed only a matter of time before his rackets would be revealed for what they were. Frankel became extremely anxious and decided to make a run for it. He assumed several false identities and hired a private jet to fly him to Europe, taking with him millions of dollars' worth of diamonds. He also took with him two of his girlfriends, who later baled out and were replaced as companions by an employee called Cynthia Allison. He hid out until he was finally found, along with Cynthia, in one of the most luxurious hotels in Hamburg, Germany. He was immediately arrested.

Indicted for fraud

Frankel was indicted by the US federal government for frauds worth over two million dollars. The German authorities also accused him of using a false passport and smuggling diamonds into the country. He pleaded guilty to the German charges, but came up with several far-fetched excuses, including the claim that he had smuggled in the diamonds so that he could feed the poor and hungry of the world. Not surprisingly, the German courts were not impressed with this story, and at his trial Frankel received a three-year sentence. While serving out his sentence, he attempted to escape from prison, but failed. In 2002, Frankel was charged with twenty-four federal counts of fraud and racketeering in the US, and finally sentenced to more than sixteen years in prison.

Frankel began to show a greedy sexual appetite and a cruel streak, surrounding himself with young women and hosting sadomasochistic orgies in the house.

Elmyr de Hory

Elmyr de Hory was one of the most talented art forgers of the twentieth century. For over two decades, his forgeries of masters such as Picasso, Matisse and Modigliani sold in their hundreds across the United States and Europe, fooling some of the greatest experts in the art world. When his fraud was discovered, the FBI and Interpol pursued him, but he managed to evade capture for most of his career. However, his life ended tragically when he committed suicide in 1976.

He was born Elmyr Dory-Boutin to a Jewish Hungarian family. His father was a diplomat, but although well-to-do, the family was an unhappy one. Elmyr spent a lot of time away from his parents, being cared for by a succession of governesses. His parents finally divorced when he was sixteen years old.

Prison camp nightmare

De Hory moved to Budapest, living among a bohemian community of artists. It was here that Elmyr began to discover his homosexual nature. When he was eighteen, he moved to Munich, Germany, enrolling in art school to study classical painting. He found that he had a real talent for the work, and went on to study in Paris under the painter Fernand Leger.

On his return to Hungary, de Hory began a relationship with a British journalist who was suspected by the Hungarian government of being a spy. As a result of this connection, he ended up in prison in the Carpathian Mountains. There, he experienced terrible conditions that were only slightly improved when he painted the portrait of a senior camp officer. Eventually, de Hory was released, but by this time the German Nazis were in control of Hungary.

As a Jew, de Hory was sent to a German concentration camp, where he was beaten so badly that he was transferred to a hospital. From there, he managed to escape, even though he had a broken leg. He then made his way back to Hungary, only to find that his parents had been killed and that most of their estate had been taken away.

Living the high life

De Hory managed to escape from Hungary to France, where he tried to start a new life. He soon found out that he had a knack for reproducing the styles of others and, in order to survive, began to sell these works. In 1946, he sold his first forgery, a Picasso, and realized that he had found a way to make a living. He began to make and sell more forgeries, claiming that the artworks had been in his family's collection.

He found a dealer, Jacques Chamberlin, and together the pair toured Europe, selling forged paintings. During this period, they lived the high

In 1946, he sold his first forgery, a Picasso, and realized that he had found a way to make a living.

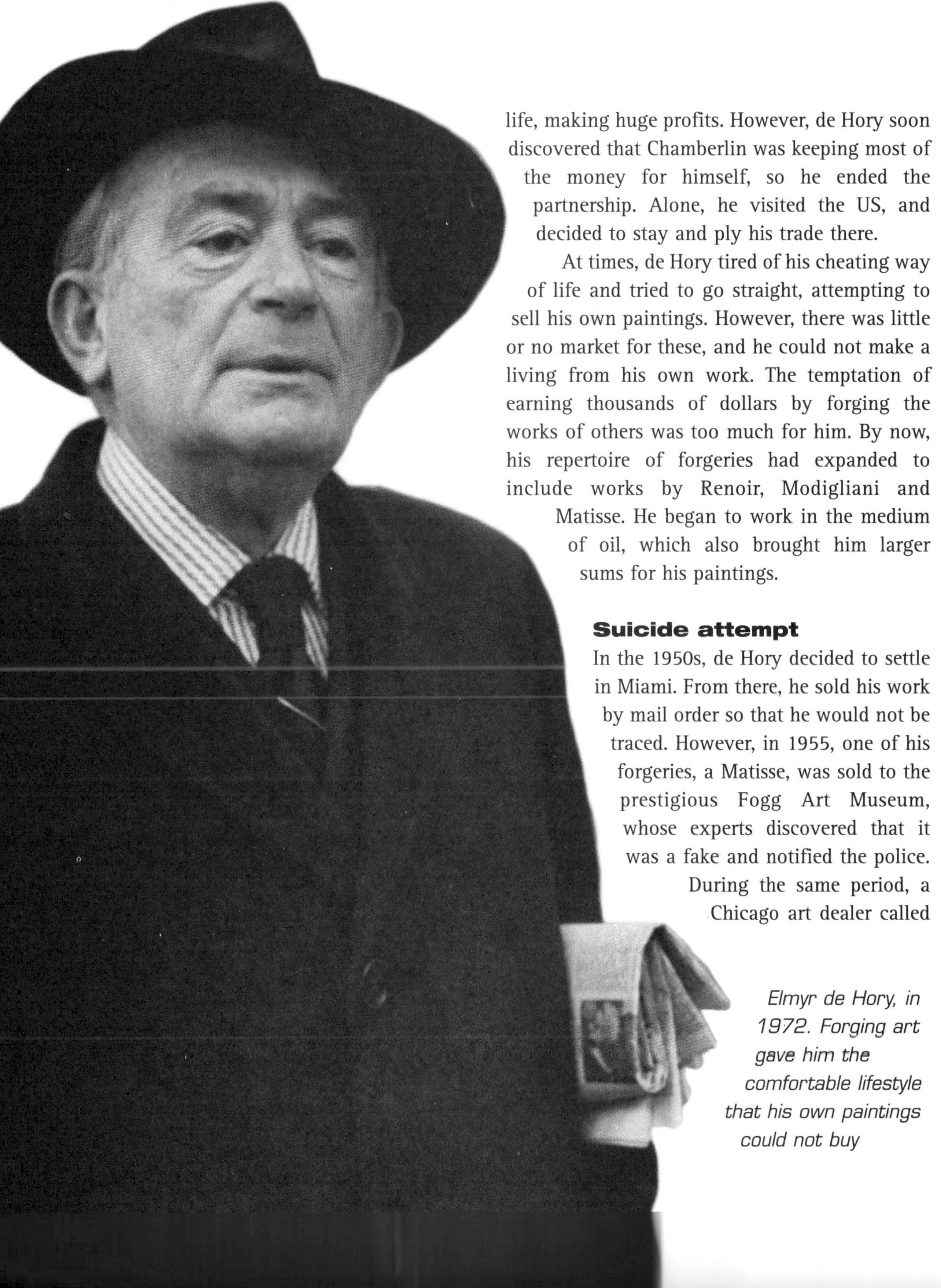

life, making huge profits. However, de Hory soon discovered that Chamberlin was keeping most of the money for himself, so he ended the partnership. Alone, he visited the US, and decided to stay and ply his trade there.

At times, de Hory tired of his cheating way of life and tried to go straight, attempting to sell his own paintings. However, there was little or no market for these, and he could not make a living from his own work. The temptation of earning thousands of dollars by forging the works of others was too much for him. By now, his repertoire of forgeries had expanded to include works by Renoir, Modigliani and Matisse. He began to work in the medium of oil, which also brought him larger sums for his paintings.

Suicide attempt

In the 1950s, de Hory decided to settle in Miami. From there, he sold his work by mail order so that he would not be traced. However, in 1955, one of his forgeries, a Matisse, was sold to the prestigious Fogg Art Museum, whose experts discovered that it was a fake and notified the police. During the same period, a Chicago art dealer called

Elmyr de Hory, in 1972. Forging art gave him the comfortable lifestyle that his own paintings could not buy

On hearing the French authorities were to extradite him, de Hory ended the struggle that was his turbulent life, and committed suicide

Joseph Faulkner found out that the works sold to him were fakes, and began a court case against de Hory. De Hory fled to Mexico City, using false papers. Here, he was unfairly jailed for the murder of a British homosexual, a crime he had not committed. After a great deal of wrangling, he was set free and returned to the US.

Back in the United States, de Hory discovered that his forgeries were selling for a lot more than he had been paid by the art galleries who bought them. He also became aware that his style of work was being recognized as fake, and worried that his source of income would soon dry up. Moreover, he was frightened of getting caught and being imprisoned again. He became depressed and took an overdose of sleeping pills. Luckily, he was discovered before he died and taken to hospital.

On his recovery, de Hory returned to Miami and there struck up a relationship with a man named Ferdinand Legros, who became his art dealer. Legros had a talent for selling, but he was dishonest, and kept most of the money from the paintings he sold. Tired of his company, de Hory left for Europe.

On the run

After several years, de Hory found that he could not make enough money on his own, and began to do business with Legros again. Legros built de Hory a splendid home on the island of Ibiza, Spain, where he could live quietly and paint in peace. However, Legros continued to swindle de Hory who, away from city life, was becoming bored. He started to produce substandard paintings and it was not long before the paintings were detected as fakes. The police embarked on the men's trails and De Hory fled to Australia, but later returned to his home in Ibiza.

In 1966, Legros sold over fifty paintings to one client, a Texas oil magnate, who later discovered that most of them were fakes. To escape the law, Legros went to Ibiza, turning de Hory out of the house. Shortly afterwards, Legros was arrested.

The final end

After trying to work in Europe, de Hory decided to give up his fugitive lifestyle and go back to Ibiza. There, the Spanish authorities charged him with homosexuality and consorting with criminals but they could not prove that he had made the forgeries on Spanish soil. De Hory spent two months in prison, and was afterwards expelled from Ibiza, though a year later he returned. By that time he was a celebrity, having appeared on television and in an Orson Wells movie, and having collaborated on a biography with writer Clifford Irving.

With his new-found fame, de Hory relaunched his career, this time selling his own paintings. However, in 1976, when he found out that the French authorities were planning to extradite him, he committed suicide, bringing his turbulent career to a final, tragic end.

Joyti De-Laurey

Joyti De-Laurey, a 35-year-old personal assistant working at the city banking firm Goldman Sachs in London, managed to con over four million pounds out of her employers before she was eventually discovered and charged with fraud. Amazingly, her bosses were so rich that for a long time they did not notice the millions missing from their accounts – but when they did, De-Laurey was arrested, charged and brought to trial. The case was sensational, and provoked a lot of controversy in Britain as the astronomical incomes of the bankers at Goldman Sachs emerged. In fact, the British newspapers often seemed to have more sympathy for De-Laurey than for the bankers who had been fleeced – causing Goldman Sachs director Edward Scott Mead to comment at one point that he felt as though he, not the defendant, was on trial.

A lesson to her employers – Joyti De-Laurey betrayed their trust, and one time took advantage of colleagues' generosity by pretending to be seriously ill

Signing cheques... to herself

De-Laurey was hired to work as a personal secretary at the prestigious investment bank of Goldman Sachs at a modest salary of around twenty thousand pounds plus bonuses – only as it turned out, the bonuses that she helped herself to were rather larger than her bosses might have expected. De-Laurey began working for super-rich banker Jennifer Moses and her husband Ron Beller, and soon made herself indispensable to both of them. She would arrange surprise birthday parties and trips abroad, book beauty sessions and do anything else that the couple required to maintain their busy, high-flying personal lifestyle. The couple were extremely grateful for De-Laurey's dedication to her job and her apparent loyalty, and trusted her completely.

Built to De-Laurey's specifications, this luxury villa in Cyprus was just one of the ill-gotten gains the PA managed to garner from her duplicity

However, unbeknown to them, their hard-working new secretary was busy forging their signatures on their cheque books, and signing cheques to herself from their bank accounts. She began with small amounts, but as her bosses seemed not to notice, the cheques got larger and larger. In four months alone, De-Laurey made over seventy forgeries to take money out of the accounts. Then she began to transfer huge amounts of money into bank accounts that she opened abroad under her maiden name. Other members of her family were also involved in the scam: her mother, a doctor; and her husband, a former chauffeur; helped her to make the transactions. They were both later convicted of money laundering.

The missing millions

During this time, De-Laurey surprised her suburban neighbours by making expensive alterations to her house and buying a fleet of luxury cars for herself, her mother and other family members. She also bought a flashy motorbike with personalized number plates for her husband Tony. She took numerous holidays, often to Cyprus, and told neighbours of her plans to buy a luxurious villa and a boat there. They assumed that she had won the lottery, but the reality was that she was operating a huge fraud from one of the biggest banks in London.

De-Laurey then thought of another way to dupe her bosses. She told them that she had cervical cancer and, out of sympathy, they arranged for her to take a trip to the United States to get specialist treatment. Instead, De-Laurey spent the money on a holiday, staying in a top Beverly Hills hotel.

Having found her bosses so co-operative, De-Laurey now began planning her retirement. She bought a villa with two swimming pools in Cyprus, costing seven hundred thousand pounds, and also ordered a luxury Italian boat for her husband, as well as a Range Rover and a custom-built Aston Martin. To pay for all this, she found

Other members of her family were also involved in the scam: her mother, a doctor; and her husband, a former chauffeur; helped her to make the transactions. They were both later convicted of money laundering.

her way into the account of Edward Scott Mead, one of Goldman Sachs' directors. Mead was an incredibly wealthy man, so much so that when she managed to transfer two million pounds from his account into her own, it took him four months to notice that the money was missing. The discovery was made when he looked at his funds to make a charity donation to his old college.

Red faces all round

When what had happened came to light, De-Laurey was arrested and charged, along with her husband and mother. After a sensational trial, in which many embarrassing details on all sides were revealed, De-Laurey was convicted and sentenced to seven years' imprisonment. Her husband and mother received shorter sentences. The furious Mead publicly branded her 'a liar and a thief' and said that she 'had violated and abused many people's trust in a most cynical and calculating way'.

The British press, however, did not always agree with this assessment. Sections of it – not only the tabloids but the quality press as well – were extremely critical of the bank, particularly of the hugely inflated salaries of its top executives. The press also had a field day in lambasting the lax way that Goldman Sachs handled its business, allowing De-Laurey to infiltrate bank accounts and embezzle money so easily. The case exposed the world of investment banking in such a way that, in the end, few had a great deal of sympathy with the bankers. Mead's personal life also came under scrutiny during the trial, as De-Laurey alleged that he had allowed her to take the money in return for covering up an affair he had been having. Mead angrily denied that he had let De-Laurey take the money, though he did admit that he was having an affair.

When De-Laurey was ordered to serve seven years in prison, many felt that her sentence was unfair – even though she was a convicted thief. The legal dealings of the business world were, some argued, not so different from what De-Laurey had done, often involving deception and abuse of trust.

Clearly, if De-Laurey had been less greedy, her thefts might never have been noticed. As a newspaper pundit wittily pointed out, Goldman Sachs' motto was: Creativity and Imagination. Perhaps their employee Joyti De-Laurey took the words somewhat too literally.

Han van Meegeren

The story of master art forger Han van Meegeren is an extraordinary one. It is likely that his forgeries would never have been discovered until after his death, had it not been for the fact that he once sold a painting – apparently by Vermeer – to the Nazi Reichsmarshall Hermann Göring during the Second World War (this was during the period when Holland was occupied by the Germans). The Dutch authorities accused van Meegeren of being a Nazi collaborator and arrested him, but he then revealed that the painting was a forgery, and that he had duped Göring into buying it. At first no one believed him, but when he managed to prove his case, he was hailed as a national hero for tricking the Nazis – instead of a traitor to his country.

Henricus Antonius van Meegeren was born in Deventer, Holland, in 1899. His parents were Roman Catholics, and he was the third child in the family. As a young man, he studied art and architecture, much to the annoyance of his father who did not approve of his son's choice of career, but van Meegeren was determined to follow in the footsteps of the classic Dutch painters – and so he did, but not in the way that he expected.

To save his life – by getting the charge of treason against him changed to forgery – van Meegeren was forced to reveal his fraudulent skills

The fake Vermeer

Unfortunately for van Meegeren, who had developed considerable skills as a painter in the classic style, the fashion of his day was for modern art. It became clear that unless he changed his direction, he was never going to be taken seriously by the critics. Indeed, when he exhibited his paintings, his work was often ridiculed. To get back at his critics, he conceived a plan that would show them up for what they

Van Meegeren explains the techniques of his last work Jesus Preaching in the Temple, *supposedly by Vermeer, but in fact produced by his own highly skilled but criminal talent*

were in his eyes: shallow, ignorant slaves to fashion who knew nothing about 'real' art. He decided to paint a fake Vermeer, watch the art world rave over it and then reveal that it was his own work. Therefore, it can be argued, that when he first took to forgery, his aim was not to make money but to show his critics his skills and techniques, thus proving what a fine painter he was.

In 1936, Han van Meegeren painted a picture of Christ at Emmaus, and passed it off as an early, unknown Vermeer. He worked very carefully, copying every aspect of Vermeer's style of painting, and using paints specially mixed according to the formulas of the period. He applied techniques that he had developed himself to glaze, harden and bake the paintings so that they appeared crackled and old, rubbing dirt into the cracks to complete the effect.

Today, scientific procedures can date a

painting accurately, however authentic it may look. However, at that time, no such methods existed, and paintings had to be judged on the basis of how they appeared to the naked eye. Van Meegeren's carefully forged Vermeer fooled the Dutch art world completely, in particular the critic Dr Abraham Bredius, whom van Meegeren loathed. Much to van Meegeren's glee, Bredius declared the painting a genuine masterpiece. Van Meegeren's trick had worked.

The black market

At this point, when van Meegeren had planned to reveal all, it became clear to him just how much money he could make by producing these fake paintings. He sold Christ at Emmaus for a huge sum; from then on, until 1945, he painted forgeries. His fake paintings by Dutch masters such as Vermeer, Pieter de Hooch and Frans Hals fetched the equivalent of millions of dollars. His forgeries remained undetected for years, and he

To get back at his critics, he conceived a plan that would show them up for what they were in his eyes: shallow, ignorant slaves to fashion who knew nothing about 'real' art.

made a great deal of money. The war raging in Europe helped cover his tracks: there was a lot of secret trafficking in works of art at the time, and his activities were not as carefully monitored as they might have been in peace time.

Van Meegeren's paintings sold for higher and higher sums. One of them cost over a million Dutch guilders, and became the most expensive painting ever sold at the time. As a result, he became used to living the high life, as one of the richest men in Holland's art world. Yet he was a difficult, unhappy man with a turbulent personal life. At heart, despite his wealth, he was still extremely bitter about his lack of success as a creative artist.

Fooling the Nazis

The last fake Vermeer that van Meegeren painted, 'Christ and the Adultress', was sold to Hermann Göring in 1943, during the Nazi occupation of Holland, for a huge sum. Two years later, at the end of the war, the painting was found in Göring's collection, and traced back to van Meegeren. Van Meegeren was arrested and charged with collaborating with the Nazis, a treasonous offence punishable by death at the time. While he was being held in prison, van Meegeren confessed that the painting, along with several others, had been forged by him. The authorities did not believe him, so to prove it, he offered to paint another fake, this time under police surveillance.

To everyone's amazement, van Meegeren was able to show that he could paint like Vermeer. He took as his subject 'Jesus Among the Doctors', and created a painting that was obviously the work of a master forger. He was duly charged with forgery rather than treason. He was so annoyed by this that he refused to finish the fake painting. At his trial, he was sentenced to prison for one year.

By this time, van Meegeren had become something of a national hero as the man who had outwitted the Nazis and divested Hermann Göring of large sums of money (in actual fact, it was later found that Göring had paid for the painting in fake currency). However, van Meegeren was not able to enjoy his moment of fame: by now he was extremely sick. Over the years, he had used his money to indulge himself, and had abused drink and drugs to such a degree that he had completely ruined his health. Instead of going to prison, he was admitted to hospital, where he died on 30 December 1947. Thus ended the bizarre career of one of the greatest master forgers in history.

Clifford Irving

Clifford Irving caused a literary storm when he wrote a fraudulent autobiography of Howard Hughes, the millionaire eccentric who, after a brilliant career in the 1950s as a movie mogul and businessman, withdrew entirely from public life. During the 1960s, Hughes became well known as a recluse, so Irving and his co-writer Richard Suskind assumed that, even with the publication of the book, their subject would not be drawn to comment on it. Unfortunately for them, they were proved wrong.

Clifford Michael Irving was born on 5 November 1930 in New York. He studied at the High School of Music and Art, and then at Cornell University. He wrote a couple of books, but neither made him any money. He kept on writing, however, marrying several times and moving to Europe during his career. In 1969 he wrote the story of an acquaintance, Elmyr de Hory, who had at one time been an infamous art forger. Irving subtitled the book *The Greatest Art Forger of Our Time*, and it became quite successful. Two years later, Irving approached his New York publisher, McGraw-Hill, with a more ambitious project: to ghostwrite the autobiography of Howard Hughes.

The millionaire recluse

Since 1958, Howard Hughes had fiercely guarded his privacy. Every time an author tried to publish a biography about him, he bought them off. By the early 1970s, he had apparently become completely paranoid about being seen in public, even refusing to make appearances in court. His extreme fear of publicity caused many to believe that he had something to hide: that he was perhaps seriously mentally ill or suffering from a terminal illness. There were even some rumours that he had actually died, and was being impersonated by someone else.

However, despite Hughes' well-known aversion to publicity, Irving managed to convince his publishers that he had somehow won the recluse's trust. He told them that he had met Hughes many times in the West Indies and in Mexico, in secret locations, and that he had

Clifford Irving – fantasist or fraudster? Did he want to believe his own tales or was he simply pulling a huge confidence trick?

recorded the whole of Hughes' autobiography on tape. To validate his claim, he forged letters from Hughes to himself, which a handwriting expert claimed to be genuine. Irving claimed that Hughes had contacted him to write the autobiography after reading his book about de Hory, and promised that the story would be an electrifying account of big business, the movie world and the aviation industry. He also said that it would detail the eccentric habits of a man so rich he could have anything that he wanted.

Obviously, a book like this seemed like a surefire bestseller. The publishers paid Irving a huge advance for the book, happy with his assurances that some of it would be paid into Howard Hughes' Swiss bank account for his role in the creation of the book.

A brilliant hoax

Irving went on to write a highly imaginative account of Hughes' life. Although in fact it was totally fabricated, and extremely far-fetched, several veteran newsmen who had interviewed Hughes in his former days as a business mogul pronounced it to be the real thing. Before the book could be published, however, Hughes – much to everyone's surprise – came out of hiding to denounce it. He used a telephone news conference to tell the world that Irving's story was completely untrue, and that it read more like a movie script than reality. Irving countered by saying that the voice on the telephone interview was a fake. He reiterated his claim that the autobiography was genuine, and was backed up by several graphologists, including the handwriting expert Paul Osborn, who said that forging so much material was 'beyond human ability'.

It was not long before Hughes' lawyers filed a law suit against Irving's publishers, McGraw Hill. An investigative reporter, James Phelan, also noticed that Irving's book contained material taken from an unpublished manuscript that he himself had written on Hughes. In addition, the Swiss bank where Irving's wife had

Despite Hughes' well-known aversion to publicity, Irving managed to convince his publishers that he had somehow won the recluse's trust.

deposited the publisher's cheque broke its rule of secrecy and revealed that the holder of the account under the name of H. R. Hughes was, in fact, a woman.

Exposed at last

Faced with the prospect of being exposed and sued for millions of dollars, the Irvings, together with co-author Richard Suskind, had to confess that the book was a hoax. They were charged with fraud, and were found guilty on 16 June 1972. Irving was made to hand back his advance to his publishers, and received a prison sentence of seventeen months. After serving his sentence, he resumed his career as a writer. He went on to write several more books, including an account of the whole affair, entitled *Hoax!*, which was published in 1981.

Count Victor Lustig

Known as 'the man who sold the Eiffel Tower – twice!', Count Victor Lustig has gone down in history as one of the greatest con men of all time. A charming yet completely corrupt swindler, he spoke five languages, went under scores of different names and was arrested many times before he was finally caught and sent to prison for good.

Victor Lustig was born in Bohemia, now the Czech Republic, on 4 January 1890. When he was nineteen, he got into a fight with a man over a girl. The man slashed his face, leaving him with a large scar that ran from his eye to his ear. When he later took to a life of crime, this was to prove a distinguishing feature.

As soon as he could, Victor left home and headed towards the bright lights of Paris. His intelligence and wit, not to mention his charm and his mastery of several languages, made it easy for him to make friends among the wealthy upper classes of Parisian society. His skill at cards led him to become a professional gambler, making a living by working on luxury ocean liners crossing from Paris to New York City. However, with the onset of the First World War, pleasure cruises like these became a thing of the past, and Lustig had to find another way to make money. He decided to travel to the United States and develop other lines of business.

Con man extraordinaire

His first major con in the US was in 1922, when he bought a dilapidated farm in Missouri, offering the bank Liberty bonds for it. The bank was only too glad to oblige, since the farm was not worth much at all, and showed its gratitude by cashing an extra ten thousand dollars of bonds for him. During the transaction, Lustig managed to switch the envelopes containing the bonds and the cash, and stole both. He was later caught, but – unbelievably – managed to persuade the bank to let him off. Not only that, but he also kept the ten thousand dollars.

His next con took place in Montreal, where he stole the wallet of a banker named Linus Merton, and then returned it to him intact, saying that he had found it. This ploy gained the banker's confidence, so Lustig told his new friend of a scheme to make money by betting on horses. In those days, racing results were wired ahead to the bookmakers several minutes before the betting was closed. Lustig told Merton that, by intercepting the wire, one could find out the winner and place a bet. He claimed that his cousin worked in the bookmaking industry and had access to this information, and that a very large bet placed on a horse at the last minute could thus be guaranteed to win. In this way, Lustig obtained thirty thousand pounds from Merton to put on a horse. Needless to say, Lustig's story was complete fiction, and once he had Merton's money, he immediately made off with it. Once again, he got away with this audacious swindle, and Merton never saw Lustig – or his money – again.

During the transaction, Lustig managed to switch the envelopes containing the bonds and the cash, and stole both. He was later caught, but – unbelievably – managed to persuade the bank to let him off.

A surprisingly jaunty Lustig, given that he had just been sentenced to a long spell in prison

An audacious scam

Lustig's third con was his most outrageous. He read a newspaper article about the Eiffel Tower being so badly in need of repair that the authorities were thinking of destroying it. Pretending to be from a government department, he sent 'official' letters to the directors of several scrap iron companies, and met with them at the Hotel de Crillon on Place de la Concorde. The Crillon was one of the best hotels in Paris, and a popular meeting place for top-level government officials. Once the gentlemen were assembled, he introduced himself as the deputy Director General of the Ministry of Posts and

Victor Lustig was as genuine a count as he was a scrap metal merchant. The title was to lend gravitas to his scams

Telegraphs. He announced that the government had decided that the upkeep of the Eiffel Tower was too expensive and that they were going to demolish it. He said that in order to secure the iron from the tower, the dealers first needed to bid for the rights to it. He then took the men for a trip around the tower, which was indeed in a bad state of repair at the time. It had never been built as a permanent structure, but as a display of engineering skill for the 1889 Paris Exposition. During the tour, Lustig noted which of the men seemed the most gullible. Afterwards, he asked that the men put forward their bids the next day, and told them to keep the project secret, since the idea of tearing down the Eiffel Tower was a very controversial one and had not been made known to the public.

Accordingly, the following day each of the companies submitted a bid for the tower. Lustig selected one of the businessmen, an unfortunate man named André Poisson, as the winner. He encouraged Poisson to bribe him, and then accepted Poisson's bid. As soon as he had the money, he went to Austria, where he enjoyed the high life in the best hotels and restaurants. He read the French newspapers every day, expecting them to report the incident and for the police to come after him, but they never did – as it turned out, Poisson was so embarrassed by his gullibility that he didn't go to the police, and the whole affair was covered up.

Pushing his luck

Encouraged by getting away with such an audacious scam, Lustig went back to Paris. He mounted exactly the same con all over again, with five new scrap iron dealers. However, this time he pushed his luck too far. The victim of the scam went straight to the police, and the story was soon reported in all the newspapers. However, the police did not manage to catch up with Lustig.

Lustig spent the remainder of his life in the United States, where he posed as a European aristocrat, calling himself 'count'. He continued to come up with a series of amazing scams, until he was finally caught, tried and sent to prison, from which he managed to make a dramatic escape, but was recaptured and sent to Alcatraz. He eventually died of pneumonia in 1947, at the age of fifty-seven.

COLD-BLOODED KILLERS

On the whole, psychotically violent killers are not very intelligent people. Many of them act from compulsions that neither they nor those around them understand. In some cases, their behaviour is linked to brain damage: a significant number of killers have at some time in their lives sustained a serious blow to the head. Others have a very limited mental capacity. But what of those killers who are intelligent, lively, charismatic people? These are the individuals that we perhaps fear most: the ones that, we feel, should have the brains to develop a moral sense; the ones who should be able to tell wrong from right, who 'should know better'. Jack Unterweger, for example, was a man from a very deprived background who educated himself in prison and, once released, became a literary celebrity; however, while he was enjoying fame and fortune as a writer, he was committing a string of murders. Again, Mark Hofmann, raised a Mormon, and a family man, turned to murder to cover his tracks when his fraudulent ways were about to be exposed. In both cases, these intelligent men deliberately chose murder as an option to maintain a lifestyle they enjoyed.

Charles Manson had the ability to attract a string of admiring followers. His childhood was very deprived, resulting in adult behaviour that was violent and mentally unstable; however, he managed to exert a strange magnetism over others, leading them to commit the most horrifying murders. What emerges from these stories is that, far from being a civilizing influence, intelligence often makes a killer all the more deadly and dangerous.

Charles Manson

Charles Manson has gone down in history as the mastermind behind a series of celebrity murders in California that shocked the United States. He and his band of followers, known as 'The Family', revealed a dark side to the hippy ideals of drugs, free love and rebellion against social convention that characterized the youth culture of Los Angeles during the 1960s and early 1970s. The seemingly amoral attitude of Manson and his followers was deeply disturbing, and to this day no simple explanation of the events that took place can be given. In particular, Manson's apparently hypnotic hold on his teenage acolytes remains a mystery. On paper, Manson had nothing to recommend him, but in person he seems to have had a strange charisma that attracted young people – especially women – to him.

Charles Milles Manson was born in 1934 to a mother who did not want him. When he was thirteen, she abandoned him. He was sent to a school for boys in Terre Haute, Indiana, but after a year he ran away and went back to his mother. She rejected him again and he began to live on the streets, scraping a living by stealing. By the time he became an adult, most of his life had been spent in prison for stealing cars, forging cheques, pimping and assault.

Helter Skelter

In 1955, he married a seventeen-year-old girl named Rosalie Jean Willis, with whom he had a baby son. Rosalie left him, with the baby, for a truck driver. Manson married again, to a woman named Leona, with whom he had another son, but the pair was soon divorced.

In 1967, after his release from jail, Manson moved to California. A small, mentally unstable man nearing forty, he nevertheless seemed to possess a considerable sexual magnetism and personal charisma. He adopted the pose of a spiritual guru, quoting from the Book of Revelation, and arguing that a race war between black and white was about to begin. He named his Armageddon philosophy 'Helter Skelter' after a Beatles song. According to Manson's tortured logic, in order to spark the race war, from which he and his followers would emerge unscathed, Family members would murder rich white people. The Family moved into an unused ranch that had once been used to make western movies. In this ghost town, he somehow convinced his

On paper, Manson had nothing to recommend him, but in person he seems to have had a strange charisma that attracted young people – especially women – to him.

Small in stature and unhealthy looking, Manson still managed to attract people, manipulating them to do his bidding

followers that the normal rules of behaviour towards fellow human beings did not apply to them. Evidently, their subsequent crimes were influenced by large amounts of mind-altering drugs, but this still did not explain why, under Manson's influence, they went on to act with such extraordinary savagery.

'Death to pigs'

On 9 August 1969, followers Susan Atkins, Charles 'Tex' Watson and Patricia Krenwinkel broke into the home of actress Sharon Tate, who was eight months pregnant at the time. Her husband, film director Roman Polanski, was away. They brutally murdered her, daubing the word 'Pig' with her blood over the door, and killing the other people who happened to be in the house. These were hairdresser Jay Sebring, coffee heiress Abigail Folger and her lover Wojciech Frykowski, and eighteen-year-old Steven Parent, who was visiting the caretaker.

The following day, businessman Leno LaBianco and his wife Rosemary were found murdered in their house. Watson, Krenwinkel and another Family member, Leslie Van Houten, had broken in and brutally strangled, stabbed and murdered them. The word 'War' was carved into Leno LaBianco's stomach with a knife and the words 'Death to pigs' and 'Helter Skelter' were daubed in blood about the house.

Naturally, the attacks provoked a horrified response, and were widely reported, especially as several of the victims were rich Californian celebrities. When the case came to trial, it emerged that there were other murders connected to these, including that of a music teacher named Gary Hinman. It also emerged that Manson may have had a crazed motive for at least some of the killings.

Revenge killings

Manson was an aspiring songwriter and singer who had at one time made friends with Dennis Wilson of the Beach Boys. The Beach Boys had recorded one of Manson's songs, and Wilson had introduced Manson to record producer Terry Melcher. Melcher had auditioned Manson for a contract but turned him down. The prosecutor's theory was that on the night of the murder, Manson had sent his followers to Melcher's house to kill him, not knowing that Melcher was away and had rented the house to Polanski and Tate. When the followers got there, they decided to kill the residents anyway.

During the trial, state-appointed defence attorney Ronald Hughes was murdered. This was widely believed to be another Family killing. Hughes had been planning to defend his client, Leslie Van Houten, by claiming that she was under the evil influence of Manson. It seems that the Family, who viewed their leader as a kind of god, had decided to take revenge on Hughes for daring to criticize Manson.

Lack of remorse

The trial itself was full of bizarre moments, such as when Atkins, Krenwinkel and Van Houten arrived at court singing and wearing party dresses; when Manson, with a large 'X'carved into his forehead, flew into a rage and threatened to cut the judge's head off; and when the women broke into Latin chant. What especially shocked onlookers, and the public at large, was the complete lack of remorse shown by the young women, especially Atkins, who laughed and joked throughout the trial, and seemed not to understand that she had committed an appallingly brutal crime.

On 25 January 1971, Manson was convicted of murder, although he had not been present at the scene of the crimes. He was sentenced to death, but later escaped the death penalty when it was outlawed in the state of California. Also convicted of murder were Krenwinkel, Atkins, Watson and Van Houten. Later, cult members Robert Beausoleil, Bruce Davis and Steve Grogan were convicted of the murders of victims Gary Hinman and Donald Shea.

Jack Unterweger

Jack Unterweger was an Austrian serial killer who achieved notoriety not only as a murderer but also as a literary celebrity. While he was committing a string of murders both in Austria and in the US, he was also enjoying fame and fortune as a writer, and even took to posing as an investigative journalist, publishing articles about the serial killer at large. Convicted of murder as a young man, and imprisoned for life, Unterweger somehow persuaded the authorities that he was a reformed character and was let out of jail, only to murder again and again until he was finally brought to justice. What had impressed the parole board was that he had worked so hard to educate himself in prison; however, his education was shown to have meant nothing in terms of improving his criminal behaviour, as was all too sadly revealed after his release.

Unterweger was born in 1952 in Austria. His mother, Theresia, was a prostitute, and he never knew his father. Theresia did not want to look after her son, and left him in the care of his grandfather, an alcoholic. The circumstances of Jack's childhood left him with a violent temper and an abiding hatred of women, especially prostitutes. As a young adult, he began to steal cars, break into houses and offices and to act as a pimp. In 1974, he raped and killed an eighteen-year-old girl called Margaret Schaefer, beating her to death and strangling her with her bra. He claimed that the victim was a prostitute, but there was little evidence to show that this was the case. Questioned by police, Unterweger confessed what had happened, adding that as he beat Schaefer, he had imagined that it was his mother he was attacking. He was brought to trial, convicted of murder and given a life sentence.

While in prison, Unterweger transformed himself from an ignorant, illiterate thug into an educated young man.

R&D

Unwilling to let him go a second time, the authorities ensured tight security for Unterweger's trial for multiple murder

Strangled with underwear

While in prison, Unterweger transformed himself from an ignorant, illiterate thug into an educated young man. He learned to read and write, edited a prison newspaper and read highbrow literature. He also began to write poems, plays and short stories, and in 1984 completed an autobiography called *Purgatory* about his life in prison. The book became a bestseller and, together with some of his other writings, helped make a name for him in the literary world. His newfound career also helped him to gain credibility as a reformed character. In 1990, after a press campaign to set him free, he was released from prison.

In the months after his release, Austria found itself in the grip of panic. A serial killer was on the loose. The killings began in 1990, when a woman named Blanka Bockova was found beaten and strangled by a river. She was not a prostitute but worked at a butcher shop in Prague, Czechoslovakia, and had last been seen in a bar, talking to a man who none of her friends knew. A few weeks later, a prostitute identified as Brunhilde Masser disappeared from her home in Graz. Not long afterwards, Heidemarie Hammerer, also a prostitute, vanished from where she lived in Bregenz. Both Masser's and Hammerer's bodies were later found; like Bockova's, the women appeared to have been strangled with their own underwear, and their bodies covered with leaves.

A blast from the past

The next victims were prostitute Elfriede Schrempf, whose body was discovered in a forest outside Graz, and four prostitutes from Vienna: Silvia Zangler, Sabine Moitzi, Regina Prem and Karin Eroglu. All the corpses were left naked, wearing only their jewellery, and all had been strangled or suffocated with their underwear. Despite mounting evidence that the murders were linked, police were reluctant to admit that a serial killer was at large, until the man who had brought Unterweger to justice for his first murder intervened.

August Schenner had by now retired, but he told the police the circumstances of Unterweger's initial conviction, and also expressed his fears that, at around the same time, Unterweger had murdered another prostitute called Marcia Horveth, whose strangled body had been discovered near Salzburg. This was a crime that Unterweger had never been charged with because he was already in jail, supposedly for life, for the murder of Schaefer.

By the time Schenner caught up with him, Unterweger had become something of a celebrity in Austria. He was making good money as a media pundit; in particular, he liked to cover stories on the Austrian serial killer, now known as 'The Courier'. He drove flashy cars, dressed snappily in white suits and was tremendously popular with women.

The educated psychopath

As the investigation began, Unterweger made a trip to Los Angeles, where shortly after his arrival three prostitutes were found strangled with their bras. American and Austrian police began to liaise, building up a powerful case against him. Aware that police were now on his trail, Unterweger and his girlfriend, eighteen-year-old Bianca Mrak, fled to Miami, where the police eventually caught up with them.

Unterweger was arrested there and later tried in Graz, Austria. In a sensational trial, he was convicted of nine murders and sentenced to life imprisonment. Shortly afterwards, he hanged himself in his cell. Thus ended the career a psychopath all the more deadly for being intelligent, educated and self-motivated.

The Menendez Brothers

Lyle and Erik Menendez shocked America when, in 1996, they planned and carried out the murder of their wealthy parents, Jose and Kitty. The young men, aged twenty-one and eighteen, paid a visit to their parents in their Beverly Hills mansion one quiet Sunday evening in 1989 and cold-bloodedly shot the pair of them while they were dozing in front of the TV. While the frenzied attack looked, at first glance, to be the work of deranged psychotic killers, it later transpired that the motive for the crime was all too rational: the brothers had murdered their parents to get their hands on their father's millions. They had plotted the murders carefully, covering their tracks so that it would look as though Jose and Kitty Menendez had been murdered in a violent housebreaking incident. However, directly after the horrific murders, the brothers came into their inheritance and began a spending spree that alerted the police. The pair was brought to trial and, despite the defence's attempts to argue that Jose Menendez had sexually abused his sons, and that they had killed in self-defence, they were both convicted of first-degree murder.

What came to light at the trial was that, although the Menendez parents had probably not sexually abused their children, they had brought them up in such a way that the boys were unable to function normally in the world, either emotionally or morally. From their earliest years, they had subjected them to tremendous pressures to achieve, and thereby not allowed them to develop their own abilities and identities. They taught them that cheating, lying and stealing was the best way to get on in the world. Jose Menendez had groomed his sons – especially his elder son, Lyle – to be as grasping, ruthless and amoral as he was, thinking that in this way they would achieve success in the business world. Unfortunately, his sons learned his values all too well – only they turned against their parents, plotting the perfect murder of their father and mother so as to inherit a fortune.

A ruthless businessman

Jose Menendez was an immigrant from Cuba, who had left his homeland after Castro came to power, and had started life in the US with very little financial or family support. Through sheer

Directly after the horrific murders, the brothers came into their inheritance and began a spending spree that alerted the police.

Well groomed and apparently well brought up, the brothers were, underneath, calculating, cold-blooded killers

hard work and determination, he had risen to become a top executive, working in a series of high-profile positions at large companies such as Hertz and RCA. In the process, he had become rich, and had gained the respect of his anglo colleagues. However, he had also made many enemies during his career, and had gained a reputation for treating his employees with contempt. He was also widely distrusted for his questionable ethics, for instance making sales figures appear better than they were by a variety of dishonest means. By the time of his death, Menendez was an extremely successful businessman; but he was not a popular one.

Family life in the Menendez home was also less rosy than it may at first have appeared. Although the family were very well-off, Kitty Menendez was not a happy woman. Her husband engaged in a series of affairs, and at home he was an oppressive presence. Kitty was depressed and angry, and she resorted to alcohol and drug abuse, often going through periods of suicidal depression. The Menendez sons also had many problems. From their earliest childhood, Jose had pushed them, overseeing every detail of their lives and making them report to him on what they did at every moment during the day. The children developed psychological problems, and began to show physical signs of stress such as bed-wetting, stomach pains and stutters. They were also both aggressive and anti-social.

Robbery and violence

Not only did Jose and Kitty pressurize their children at home, they also refused to accept that they were anything but brilliant at school. Neither child showed much academic talent, yet their parents insisted that they should excel. Jose harboured an ambition for Lyle to attend an Ivy League College as he himself had never had the opportunity to go to one. One result of this was that Kitty began to do the children's homework for them, making sure that they got high grades, and at the same time teaching them that it was acceptable to cheat in order to succeed. Later, when Lyle did in fact manage to get to Princeton – mainly because of his skill at tennis – he was suspended for a year for plagiarism.

By the time Lyle and Erik were teenagers, their behaviour had spiralled out of control. They had taken to robbing their neighbours, stealing cash and jewellery, and had been arrested for the crimes. Jose had intervened and managed to pay off the authorities. Used to being protected by their parents, the boys seemed to have no conception that what they had done was wrong, and continued their arrogant, violent behaviour both at home and in the outside world. Kitty had become frightened of them, and had taken to sleeping with guns in her bedroom.

Bodies riddled with bullets

As it turned out, she was right to be frightened. The brothers eventually turned on their own parents one night, gunning them down in cold blood. They repeatedly shot their father, and then their mother, at one point running out to their car to fetch more ammunition so that they could finish off the job. Afterwards, when the bodies were riddled with bullets and covered in blood, the brothers telephoned for help. When police arrived on the scene, they told them that they had discovered the bodies when they came home that night. They were believed, yet those who knew the family had their suspicions.

It was not long before Lyle and Erik began to throw their parents' money around. They took rooms in luxury hotels, rented expensive apartments, and spent huge amounts on cars, clothes, and jewellery. Lyle tried to go into business, setting up a chain of restaurants, but it soon became clear that he did not have the remotest idea of what he was doing. Erik decide to become a professional tennis player, but he too seemed to be living in a fantasy land.

Soon, the pressure became too much for Erik and he confessed his part in the murders to his therapist, Jerome Oziel. Furious at this, Lyle threatened Oziel, but Oziel did not report him to the police. Later, Oziel's testimony was used at the trial. The complications of the case meant that the preparation for the trial dragged on for three years, during which time the brothers were held in custody. However, the evidence against them was eventually found to be overwhelming, and they were both sentenced to life in prison. Today, they continue to serve out their sentences.

Mark Hofmann

Mark Hofmann has been called 'one of the most chillingly compelling criminals the world has ever known'. In 1997 he forged a poem, by the nineteenth-century American poet Emily Dickinson, which completely fooled the literary world. However, his greed finally got the better of him; to finance his lifestyle, he borrowed money to create yet more forgeries to sell and, when he could not pay back the money, ended up murdering two victims. When arrested, Hofmann confessed to many forgeries, as well as the murders, and at his trial received a life sentence. Today, he remains incarcerated in the Utah State Correctional Facility.

Hofmann was born in 1954 and grew up in a devout Mormon family, living in the suburbs of Salt Lake City. As a child, he was interested in chemistry and in performing magic tricks. At the age of fourteen, he managed to electroplate an 'antique' coin in such a way that the US Treasury department declared it to be genuine. These childhood hobbies would serve him well in his later career as a master forger.

A typical Mormon image by C. C. A. Christensen showing the angel Moroni – and not a salamander – revealing the word of God to Joseph Smith

The Salamander Letter

Early on, Hofmann began to doubt his family's faith. He came to believe that the founder of the Mormon religion, Joseph Smith, was a fraud. Smith had claimed that his teachings, compiled as The Book of Mormon, were given to him by an angel called Moroni, and that he, Smith, had transcribed them from a set of golden plates using 'magic goggles'. To suggest that these claims were false, Hofmann set about recreating a page of Smith's work. He treated paper and ink to look as though they were from the nineteenth century, adding every detail expected of an old book. Later, when the forgery was tested, the page was declared genuine.

Buffalo, N.Y. at 8 o'clock
A.M. and arrived at home
Monday, the 4th at 10 A.M.
found my family all well
according to the promise
of the Lord. for which
blessings I feel to thank
his holy name. Amen
November 13th nothing
of note transpired from
the 4th of Noveber util this
day in the morning at 4
O'clock I was awoke by
Brother Davis knocking at
my door saying Brother Joseph
come get up and see the signs in
the heavens and I arose and
beheld to my great joy the
stars fall from heaven yea
they fell like hail stones a
litteral fulfillment of the
word of God as recorded in
the holy scriptures and a
sure sign that the coming
of Christ is close at hand
Oh how marvellous are thy
works Oh Lord and I thank
thee for thy mercy unto me
thy servent Oh Lord
save me in thy kingdom
for Christ Sake Amen

He developed a method of hypnotizing himself before writing, so that he could think himself into each character, identifying himself completely with his chosen subject.

Hofmann then began to create forgeries that would cast further doubt on the Mormon religion, such as a letter from Joseph Smith, called 'The Salamander Letter'. In this, Smith apparently admitted that he had been shown the Book of Mormon by a salamander, and not the angel Moroni. In order to protect themselves and the religious beliefs of fellow Mormons, elders of the Mormon faith began to buy Hofmann's documents. From this point on, Hofmann realized that he could make a lot of money from his forgeries, and began his new career in earnest.

Fooling the experts

Hofmann had an extraordinary ability to adopt the writing style of just about any historical figure he wanted to, from George Washington to Mark Twain. He developed a method of hypnotizing himself before writing, so that he could think himself into each character, identifying himself completely with his chosen subject.

One of Hofmann's most notorious stunts was to forge a poem by the reclusive nineteenth-century poet Emily Dickinson. Amazingly, he wrote a new poem in her unique literary style, reproducing her handwriting exactly. Through meticulous historical research, as well as self-hypnosis, he managed to see into her mind and produce a remarkable new piece of writing. Not only the words of the poem itself, but his painstaking attention to technical detail ensured that the manuscript he created fooled the greatest experts in the country. The poem thrilled the literary world, and was pronounced genuine. It was bought by the library at Amhurst, Dickinson's home town, for over twenty thousand dollars.

One of Joseph Smith's genuine diaries. Forging similar documents would have taken a lot of

An enduring mystery

Hofmann's downfall came when he began to get entangled in money problems. To complete more forgeries, he borrowed half a million dollars that he could not pay back. He was also an avid collector of first editions of children's books – an expensive hobby. The volume of 'finds' he was making began to cause suspicion and his (forged) documents were subject to more and more scrutiny. As his creditors began to pursue him, he resorted to planting bombs. He murdered document collector Steven Christensen, who owned a forged document that he had bought for one million dollars from Hofmann, as well as the wife of Christensen's employer. When another bomb went off prematurely and wounded Hofmann himself, an investigation was launched, which soon led to the discovery of forgery equipment in his basement. Hofmann was arrested, charged, and received a life sentence. His extraordinary ability to recreate the minds, and create works, of some of the greatest figures in American history led to feats unsurpassed in audacity to this day.

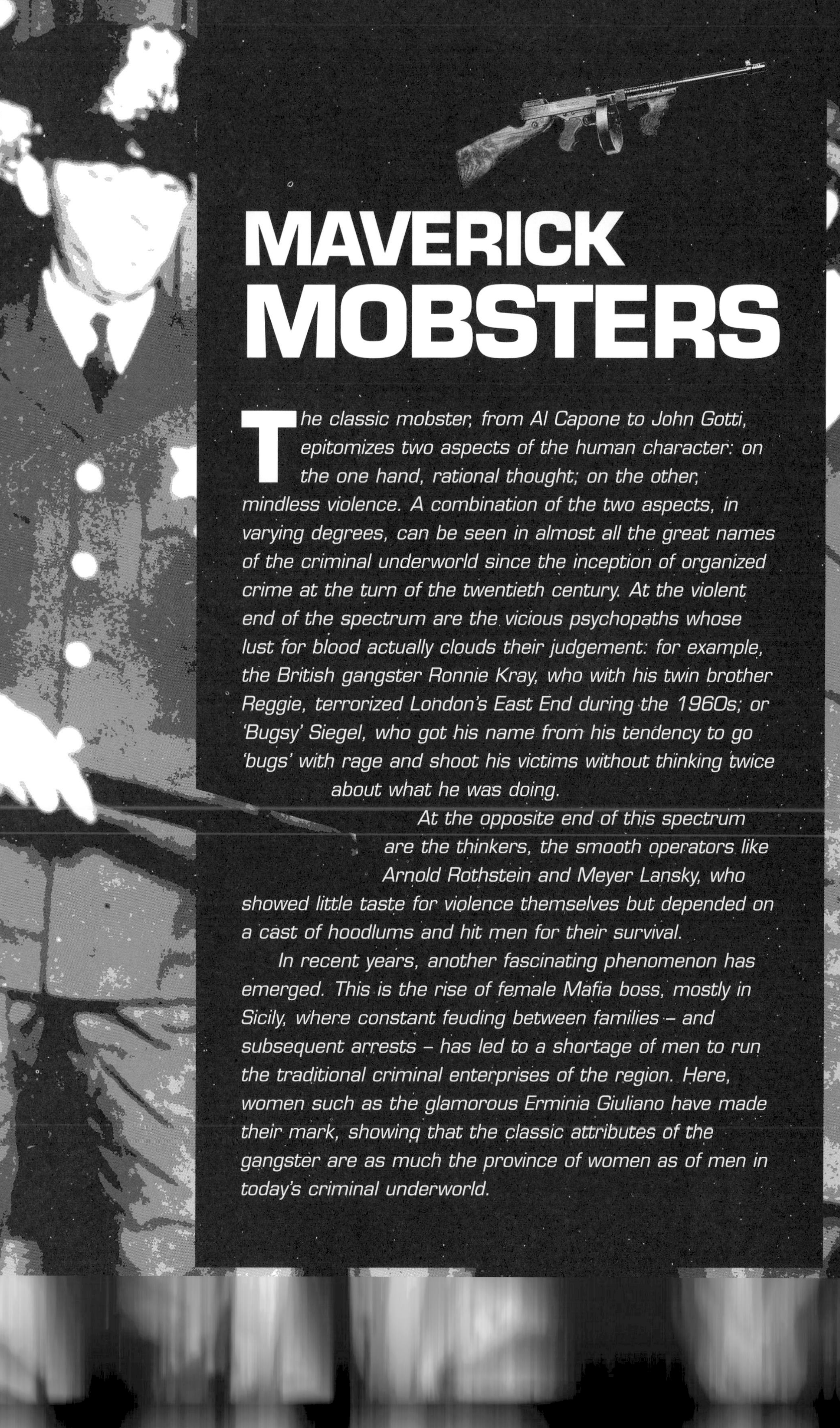

MAVERICK MOBSTERS

The classic mobster, from Al Capone to John Gotti, epitomizes two aspects of the human character: on the one hand, rational thought; on the other, mindless violence. A combination of the two aspects, in varying degrees, can be seen in almost all the great names of the criminal underworld since the inception of organized crime at the turn of the twentieth century. At the violent end of the spectrum are the vicious psychopaths whose lust for blood actually clouds their judgement: for example, the British gangster Ronnie Kray, who with his twin brother Reggie, terrorized London's East End during the 1960s; or 'Bugsy' Siegel, who got his name from his tendency to go 'bugs' with rage and shoot his victims without thinking twice about what he was doing.

At the opposite end of this spectrum are the thinkers, the smooth operators like Arnold Rothstein and Meyer Lansky, who showed little taste for violence themselves but depended on a cast of hoodlums and hit men for their survival.

In recent years, another fascinating phenomenon has emerged. This is the rise of female Mafia boss, mostly in Sicily, where constant feuding between families – and subsequent arrests – has led to a shortage of men to run the traditional criminal enterprises of the region. Here, women such as the glamorous Erminia Giuliano have made their mark, showing that the classic attributes of the gangster are as much the province of women as of men in today's criminal underworld.

Al Capone

Al Capone, a.k.a. Scarface, is perhaps the most famous of all gangsters. His name sums up an era when organized crime looked set to take over America. This was the 1920s when Prohibition created a huge money-making industry under the control of criminal gangs, giving them unimaginable wealth. Nowhere was the wealth and power more obvious than in Chicago, where the mob's front man was Al Capone. For many years, he appeared to be above the law, murdering his enemies while the police looked the other way. The legend of Scarface became known across the world, and such was his fame that he became the subject of many books and films.

Remarkably, more than half a century after his death, his name remains a byword for the urban gangster, vividly remembered today while most of his contemporaries are forgotten. The reason? Perhaps it is the mixture of calculation and brutality that he embodied. Al Capone was both a conscientious book-keeper and a man capable of beating another human being to death with a baseball bat: in short, the ultimate gangster.

An equal opportunities gangster

There was little in Al Capone's childhood to suggest such an outcome. He was born Alphonse Capone in New York on 17 January 1899, the fourth child of Gabriele and Teresina Capone, Italian immigrants from a small

The classic look of Al Capone – a mobster who once appeared on the cover of Time *magazine*

While working there, Capone got involved in a dispute with a gangster named Frank Gallucio that ended with Capone getting cut three times across the face. These were the wounds that led to his nickname: Scarface.

town near Naples who had arrived in New York five years before. The Capones were hard-working people, better off than many of their fellow immigrants. Gabriele was a barber by trade and able to read and write: he got a job first as a grocer and then, once he had saved some money, he opened his own barbershop. Soon after Alphonse was born, the family was able to move out of the Italian ghetto where they had initially lived to a more prosperous multi-ethnic area. Growing up in such a neighbourhood was no doubt responsible for the fact that, later on, Capone was unusual among Italian gangsters for his lack of ethnic, or even racial, prejudices.

Al Capone did reasonably well at school until the age of fourteen when he had a fight with a teacher. He was expelled from school and started to hang out on the streets, where he came into the orbit of local gangster Joseph Torrio. Capone joined Torrio's outfit, the James Street Gang, and later went on to become part of the Five Points Gang, along with a childhood friend, and fellow future mob boss, 'Lucky' Luciano.

Torrio moved his operation to Chicago in 1909 and, for a time, Capone worked at regular jobs until Frankie Yale, a friend of Torrio, offered Capone a job as bartender in the Harvard Tavern on Coney Island. While working there, Capone got involved in a dispute with a gangster named Frank Gallucio that ended with Capone getting cut three times across the face. These were the wounds that led to his nickname: Scarface.

The rise of Scarface

Not long after this incident, Capone met a girl called Mae Coughlan from a middle-class Irish family. In 1918 they had a child, Alphonse Jr (known as Sonny) and married the following year. Once again, Al straightened out and got a job as a book-keeper in Baltimore. Then, in November 1920, his father Gabriele died, which seemed to prompt Al to give up any pretence of living the straight life.

Capone moved to Chicago and hooked up with Johnny Torrio. The Chicago boss at the time was a man named Big Jim Colosimo, whose main business was running brothels, but now that Prohibition had come into force, Torrio could see that the big money was in illicit liquor. Colosimo was not interested in pursuing this line of business. As far as Torrio and Capone were concerned, this meant that he was in the way. Torrio arranged alibis for himself and Capone, and hired his old friend Frankie Yale from New York to shoot Colosimo down in his own night-club on 11 May 1920.

The Capone gang did not disband after Al Capone was jailed; it simply carried on under the leadership of the Fischetti brothers, the Guzik clan and Tony Accardo

As a result of this take-over bid, Torrio was now the big man in the Chicago rackets, with Capone as his right-hand man. Over the next few years, their gang made huge profits through bootlegging, but they also made many enemies among rival mobsters, notably Dion O'Banion, leader of the Irish North Side Gang. Once again, Torrio and Capone called upon the services of Frankie Yale, who shot O'Banion down during 1924. This inevitably provoked a backlash and, when Torrio himself was badly wounded in an assassination attempt the following year, he decided to give up the business. He passed control of his businesses, which by then amounted to thousands of whorehouses, gambling joints and speakeasies, to his protégé Al Capone.

St Valentine's Day Massacre

Despite being only twenty-five years old, Capone relished the new responsibility. He was an effective leader, able to build bridges with other gangs thanks to his lack of prejudice against working with Jewish or Irish gangsters. However, those who did try to challenge him paid very high penalties. One vendetta was with an Irish gang led by Bugs Moran and culminated in the so-called St Valentine's Day Massacre.

Capone's plan was to lure Moran and his gang to a meeting where they expected to make a deal for some bootleg whiskey. Fake police would then show up and disarm the Moran gang, then shoot them dead. Everything went according to plan: seven of the Moran gang were tricked by the fake officers, who lined them up against a wall and machine gunned them, killing six on the spot. The only flaw was that Moran himself arrived late to the meet and thus escaped.

Capone was not personally involved in the massacre but soon after, when two of the gangsters used on that occasion, John Scalise and Albert Anselmi, were suspected of changing sides, Capone was very much present at their execution. The two men were invited to a grand banquet in their honour. At the end of the meal, Capone was presented with a gift-wrapped parcel containing a baseball bat. While his bodyguards restrained the two men, Capone used the bat to beat them both to death.

Caught... for tax evasion

Such excesses could not carry on indefinitely. Up to this point, Capone had avoided prosecution by paying off police and politicians alike. In the Chicago township of Cicero where he lived, he had his men elected to run the place. However, the FBI, now under the direction of the legendary Elliot Ness, had a new weapon that they were starting to use against gangsters: charging them with tax evasion on their ill-gained funds. Eventually, with the help of informant Frank O'Hare, Ness managed to make a case against

Capone. It took years of skirmishes between the two men, but in the end Ness won.

In 1931, Capone was convicted of several charges of tax evasion and sentenced to eleven years in prison. Much of this was spent in the notorious Alcatraz. By the time he was released in 1939, Capone was a broken man, his health – both physical and mental – ruined by jail and the effects of long-untreated syphilis. He retired to his Florida mansion, and died on 25 January 1947.

Al Capone in custody – the only crime the prosecutors could pin on Capone was tax evasion

John Gotti

The final arrest of John Gotti marked the end of an era in organized crime. He was the last of the old-style Mafia bosses to become a household name. Gotti was the product of a media age in which fascination with the Mafia was at an all-time high, and the media was desperate to find a real life counterpart to the godfathers of popular films. They came up with John Gotti, a well-dressed *capo* with a nice repertoire of one-liners.

Gotti was born on 27 October 1940. He was the fifth of eleven children born to John Gotti Sr and his wife, Fannie. At the time of John's birth, the family lived in the poverty-stricken South Bronx. By the time he was ten, they managed to move to Sheepshead Bay in Brooklyn, and then, a year or so later, to another Brooklyn neighbourhood, East New York.

Every inch the old style Mafia boss, Gotti rarely lost his composure, even when sentenced to a term in a prison with a notoriously harsh regime

The Fulton-Rockaway Boys

Growing up, Gotti was drawn to the criminal lifestyle he saw around him. By the time he was twelve, he was running errands for local mobsters, forming a gang with his brothers Peter and Richard. John soon quit going to school and concentrated on getting into trouble instead. When he was fourteen, he crushed his toes while attempting to steal a cement mixer and spent several months in hospital, before being released with a limp he would have for the rest of his life.

Aged sixteen, Gotti became a member of a Brooklyn street gang called the Fulton-Rockaway Boys, who prided themselves on being serious criminals. They stole cars and fenced stolen goods. Other members of the gang included two associates who would stay with Gotti through most of his career, Angelo Ruggiero and Wilfred 'Willie Boy' Johnson. Between 1957 and 1961, Gotti was arrested five times, but managed to avoid prison each time.

In 1960, when he was twenty, Gotti met Victoria Di Giorgio. They had their first child, Angela, a year later, and got married the following year on 6 March 1962. The couple remained together until Gotti died, and had five children, but the marriage proved to be a stormy one, with many fights and periods of separation.

Cigarettes and stockings

Following his marriage, Gotti briefly tried his hand at legitimate employment, working for a trucking company before opting instead for a full-time life of crime. He served a brief jail

sentence in 1963 when he was caught with Salvatore Ruggiero, Angelo's younger brother, in a stolen car. This was followed by another short jail sentence in 1966, this time for robbery. That same year, Gotti joined a Mafia gang operating out of a club in Queens. This gang was part of the Gambino family, controlled by Carlo Gambino and his underboss, Aniello Dellacroce.

Gotti's particular role in the organization was as a hijacker, specializing in stealing loads from John F. Kennedy airport. Several more arrests followed as Gotti was caught with truckloads of women's clothing and cigarettes. Eventually, he spent three years in the federal penitentiary in Lewisburg for hijacking. When he was released in January 1972, he immediately returned to the Bergin gang. Soon he became the effective *capo* of the crew, with the approval of Dellacroce. Times were changing and, despite the Mafia's previous policy of having nothing to do with selling drugs, it was becoming increasingly clear that there was big money to be made in this area.

Gotti's next step up the ladder came as the result of a spate of kidnappings that broke out among Mafiosi during the early 1970s. In one incident, Carlo Gambino's nephew was kidnapped and murdered. A known kidnapper, James McBratney, was suspected. Gotti was one of three men who gunned McBratney down in a Staten Island diner soon afterwards.

Shoot-out at the steakhouse

Gotti was identified by witnesses, but the charge was bargained down to manslaughter and he served only two years of it. While Gotti was in prison, Carlo Gambino died, leaving another mobster named Paul Castellano in his place, while Dellacroce remained as the underboss.

He assembled a team of hit men and, on 16 December 1985, Paul Castellano was assassinated as he left a Manhattan steakhouse. Afterwards, Gotti moved quickly to take his position at the head of the Gambino family.

Gotti became increasingly disenchanted with the leadership of the remote Castellano. He agitated for Dellacroce to be given the job instead, but Dellacroce, who was by now suffering from cancer, counselled Gotti to have patience. Meanwhile, in 1980, personal tragedy struck the Gotti family. A neighbour, John Favara, accidently ran over and killed the Gottis' twelve-year-old son, Frank. Four months later, following a series of death threats, Favara was abducted by four men and never seen again, though rumours as to his fate abounded.

FBI surveillance of the Gambino family intensified during the 1980s, and tensions between rival leaders increased as a result. In 1985, Dellacroce finally died of cancer. Gotti was hoping to be made the new underboss by Castellano. When it became clear that Castallano intended to promote Thomas Bilotti instead, Gotti decided it was time to act. He assembled a team of hit men and, on 16 December 1985, Paul Castellano was assassinated as he left a Manhattan steakhouse. Afterwards, Gotti moved quickly to take his position at the head of the Gambino family.

The Teflon Don

Following this sensational murder, reminiscent of the old days of Mafia feuds, Gotti became a kind of alternative celebrity. Time and again the FBI would arrest Gotti on one charge or another, and time and again he would appear in court in an immaculately tailored suit and beat the rap. During this period, he acquired a series of nicknames. First he was called 'The Dapper Don' in honour of his sharp suits, then 'The Teflon Don' in recognition of the FBI's seeming inability to lay a glove on him despite near-constant surveillance. Gotti became well known for conducting meetings while walking down the street or playing recordings of white noise to prevent any bugs from working. However, by now the FBI were locked in a battle they could not be seen to lose. In 1992, they once again brought racketeering charges against Gotti under the RICO legislation, and this time they found a weak point.

The 'Teflon Don' had the silver tongue of a politician – perhaps a role he could have played had he not chosen a life of crime

Gotti's underboss was a notoriously brutal mobster named Sammy 'The Bull' Gravano, a man believed to be responsible for at least nineteen murders. So desperate were the FBI to convict Gotti that they offered Gravano, a known killer, a virtual free pass in return for testifying against his boss. To secure the deal,

they played Gravano tapes of Gotti making disparaging remarks about him. A livid Gravano agreed to testify against his boss, making him one of the highest-ranking mobsters ever to turn informer.

The don goes down

Gravano's testimony was sufficient to see Gotti finally put behind bars. He was convicted on 2 April 1992 for fourteen counts of murder, conspiracy to commit murder, loan sharking, racketeering, obstruction of justice, illegal gambling and tax evasion. To punish this highly public criminal even more, he was sent to the federal penitentiary in Marion Illinois, where he was kept in solitary confinement for 23 hours a day until his death from cancer on 10 June 2002. Meanwhile, Sammy 'The Bull' Gravano remains within the safety of the witness protection programme to this day.

Lucky Luciano

Although given his nickname when quite young, Luciano was indeed lucky – dying of natural causes is a rare way for a Mafia mobster to go

One of the most influential Mafia bosses of the twentieth century, 'Lucky' Luciano almost single-handedly transformed the world of organized crime from a few warring Italian families to a large number of affiliated ethnic groups running criminal activities on a grand scale. A vicious killer who was finally jailed for running one of the biggest prostitution rings of all time in the US, he was also an intelligent, able businessman, and a patriotic American to boot. The contradictions of his life were such that, while serving a prison sentence for his crimes, he also helped the American government in the war effort during the Second World War.

He was born Salvatore Lucania in Lercara Friddi, a village near Corleone in Sicily. When he was ten years old, he moved with his family to the US. He began his career of crime early, demanding that younger children playing on the streets pay him a cent a day to protect them from older ones. Children who refused to pay were given a sound thrashing. One of those who refused protection was the young Meyer Lansky, who put up a good fight when Luciano attacked him. Lansky went on in later years to become a top Mafia boss like Luciano, and the pair became friends.

Throat cut

As a young man, Luciano joined a team of thugs known as the Five Points Gang, headed by John Torrio. Members of the gang were suspected by local police of being involved in many crimes, including murder. Luciano specialized in pimping and in protection rackets; he also dealt heroin on the streets. It was not long before his ruthless spirit of enterprise attracted the

Gangsters cut his throat and threw him in a ditch, thinking that he was dying or dead. Amazingly, he survived, and was known by the nickname of 'Lucky' for the rest of his life.

attention of the most influential mobsters in New York, such as Vito Genovese and Frank Costello. He began working for them, and soon became a leading member of one of the biggest Mafia families in the US, the Masserias, organizing prostitution, bootlegging, drug trafficking and other criminal activities.

At the end of the 1920s, Joe 'The Boss' Masseria became embroiled in a gang war with Salvatore Maranzano, leader of another important Italian mobster family. During this period, Luciano was captured by Maranzano's men as he waited for a shipment of drugs at the docks in New York. His mouth was taped shut and he was driven out to Staten Island. There, the gangsters cut his throat and threw him in a ditch, thinking that he was dying or dead. Amazingly, he survived, and was known by the nickname of 'Lucky' for the rest of his life.

Dead men's shoes

The incident prompted Luciano to become even more ambitious. Already, he had broken with several of the traditional ways of doing business among the Mafia. For example, he associated openly with gangsters from other ethnic groups, an innovation to which his boss Masseria was deeply opposed. Luciano had close links with two major Jewish gangsters, Meyer Lansky and 'Bugsy' Siegel; later, this threesome was to form the National Crime Syndicate, with Luciano as the originator, Lansky as the brains and Siegel as the brawn.

For now, however, Luciano had to operate within the constraints of the old-time Mafia bosses. The only way to change the situation, he realized, was to kill off the top men. When Maranzano began to gain the upper hand in the turf war, he switched sides and, together with Siegel, arranged for Masseria's murder. Within six months, however, he was plotting against his new boss, Maranzano. Maranzano was duly dispatched with ruthless efficiency. Now, with both the big men out of the way, the field was clear for Luciano and his men to take the lead.

Luciano went on to head the Mafia and to restructure the world of organized crime. Instead of continuing with the old gang wars, he divided up different areas of crime between the major families, including families who were not of Italian origin. He then developed a system where, when problems arose, he could balance the interests of all concerned. Luciano was one of the first Mafia bosses to realize the obvious fact that, at the end of the day, all criminals have one common interest: to make the maximum amount of money in the shortest time possible, whatever the means might be.

Although at home on the streets of Sicily, Luciano considered the US to be his first home

The fall of the Luciano empire

To this end, the National Crime Syndicate, as Luciano's organization now became known, formed a commission with a board of directors, whose job it was to regulate the criminal underworld. These included such major mobster figures as Meyer Lansky, Joe Adonis, 'Dutch' Schultz, Louis Lepke and Frank Costello. The commission also provided a variety of services to its members, including a professional hitman service known as Murder Inc.

Luciano inevitably fell foul of the law. He was vigorously pursued and finally prosecuted by the US Attorney of New York, Thomas E. Dewey, and ended up serving a long prison sentence for running a huge prostitution ring. However, while he was in jail, an unusual opportunity came up for him. He was asked by the US government to help them plan their invasion of Sicily, using his connections with the world of underground crime there to aid the Allies. As a reward, he was given parole, on condition that he return to Italy.

Murder plots

Luciano was very upset about having to leave the US, which he considered his homeland. He did not stay long in Italy, but went to Cuba, where he began to organize a crime syndicate. However, when the US authorities found out what he was doing, he was forced to return to Italy. There, he continued to be involved in Mafia activities, running the criminal underworld of New York from afar. During this time, he became the target of a murder plot and also plotted the murder of several other Mafia bosses.

In 1962, he died of a heart attack while at the airport in Naples. His body was flown to New York City, where he was buried at St John's Cemetery in Queens. A court ruled that, since he was now a corpse, he was not a citizen of any country, and that therefore deportation rules no longer applied to him. Thus, in death – though not in life – he finally found his final resting place in the country that he had always thought of as home.

The Kray Twins

The Kray Twins masterminded the world of organized crime in London's East End during the 1960s. Their fearsome reputation for ruthless violence protected them from the law for many years, but in the end they were arrested, convicted of murder and sentenced to life imprisonment. Both of them later died while serving their sentences. Although they were both vicious criminals, they have often been depicted as 'rough diamonds', essentially good-hearted cockney characters who kept a certain amount of law and order in the East End underworld – but their law and their order. The demise of their reign of terror coincided with the fragmenting of the close-knit, colourful East End community at the end of the 1960s, which perhaps explains why these legendary villains have been sentimentalized to such a degree by the popular media, both in Britain and internationally.

Dodging the draft

Ronald and Reginald, or Ronnie and Reggie as they were known, were born in 1933. Their father, Charlie, was seldom at home, but travelled the country as a trader, knocking at people's doors to buy and sell goods. Although he was a hard drinker and gambler, he earned a good living, and made sure that his family lived well. His wife, Violet, and his children were always comfortably housed, clothed and fed, and the children were surrounded by a close network of relatives and neighbours. As well as the twin boys Ronnie and Reggie, there was an older brother, Charlie, who often took responsibility for his younger brothers in the absence of their father.

When Charlie Snr was called up to fight in the Second World War, he repeatedly dodged the draft, which meant that military police often called at his home to find him. This situation

Ronnie and Reggie, with their beloved mum, Violet

gave the brothers a lifelong hatred of authority that was later to become a hallmark of their criminal behaviour.

Armed robberies and arson attacks

In their early days at school, both twins were co-operative pupils. Encouraged by their grandfather, Jimmy 'Cannonball' Lee, they took up amateur boxing and did well at it. However, the pastime spurred them to fight constantly on the streets, and they became known as notorious bullies among the youth of the East End. In 1951, the pair was called up for state military training, or National Service as it was called, but like their father, they were unwilling to become soldiers. They both escaped from army camp several times, and eventually ended up in military prison for assaulting a police officer who noticed that they were on the run and tried to arrest them. They were imprisoned for the assault, but behaved so badly that eventually they were given a dishonourable discharge from the army.

As a result of their anti-social behaviour, the twins now had few career options. They bought a nightclub in Bethnal Green, in the East End, and from there ran a variety of criminal enterprises, including protection rackets, armed robberies and arson attacks for insurance claims. The operation expanded quickly, and more gang members were brought in. However, as it transpired later during their trial, their empire could have been much bigger and more efficient had they not argued with each other constantly.

A close-knit family – Reggie, Charles Jr and Ronnie Kray

A reign of terror

Even so, through their many nefarious activities the Krays became rich, and went on to acquire several more nightclubs. The clubs became part of the newly emerging 'swinging London' scene of the 1960s. Ronnie in particular enjoyed having his photo taken with celebrities of the day, and in this way the twins started to become famous, not only within the East End, but

Savile Row-suited London gangsters Ronnie and Reggie Kray walking along an East End street, London, 1965

nationally. As a homosexual, Ronnie made friends with several high-profile figures of the day, including Lord Boothby, a high-ranking Conservative, who was the centre of a tabloid scandal at that time.

As the Krays' fame and fortune increased, so did their criminal activities. However, it was difficult for the police to get witnesses to testify against the brothers, because of their increasing reputation for violence. Ronnie in particular was feared by everyone in the East End. He was by this time suffering from mental illness, and was brutally savage in his attacks on rival gangsters, informers and others. It was only when the pair started to turn on their own followers that the law was able to catch up with them.

Stabbed to death

In 1967, Reggie killed a member of the Kray gang, Jack 'The Hat' McVitie, so called because he always wore a hat to cover a bald patch in the middle of his head. A minor player in the Krays' gang, McVitie was a seedy drunkard who often criticized the twins, disobeyed orders and generally refused to be intimidated by his bosses. To punish him, members of the gang lured him to a house in the East End, where they stabbed him to death.

Inspector Leonard 'Nipper' Read of Scotland Yard had been trying to bring down the Krays for several years, but only now did he begin to get incriminating statements from witnesses about the brothers' activities. In 1968, Scotland Yard managed to build up enough evidence to arrest the twins and several important members of 'The Firm', as their gang was known. As the police had hoped, once the Krays and their henchmen were in custody, many more witnesses came forward to testify against them.

Psychotic cruelty

After a long trial at the Old Bailey in London, the twins were both convicted of murder and given life sentences. Several other men from 'The Firm' were also found guilty of murder: John 'Ian' Barrie, Tony Lambrianou, Christopher Lambrianou, and Ronnie Bender. The Krays' elder brother Charlie and two other men were found guilty of being accessories to the murder of Jack McVitie.

During the trial, the psychotic cruelty of the twins came to light. As well as the murder of McVitie, Ronnie had shot dead a man named George Cornell at the Blind Beggar public house in the East End, in full view of all the customers, for calling him 'a fat poof'. (No witnesses to this murder ever came forward until the twins were in custody, so terrified were they of the consequences.) Reggie was also shown to be an extremely violent man, though most often committing his crimes as a result of Ronnie's influence. In the McVitie murder, Reggie had repeatedly stabbed the victim in the face, neck and stomach, while being urged on by Ronnie, who was holding the victim down.

The death of the Krays

Ronald Kray died in 1995 in a mental institution, having been certified insane. Reginald was let out of prison in 2002 on compassionate grounds because he had terminal cancer, but he died the same year. Thus the career of the Kray twins, once feared throughout the London underworld, finally came to an ignominious end.

After a long trial at the Old Bailey in London, the most expensive ever held there up to that time, the twins were both convicted of murder and given life sentences.

Meyer Lansky

Meyer Lansky was one of the key figures in the formation of the US Mafia, responsible for transforming black-market activities such as bootlegging, prostitution and narcotics trafficking into an organized crime syndicate spanning America. He is credited with the remark that the National Crime Syndicate, as it became known, was 'bigger than US Steel'. Many commentators have speculated that, had Lansky had a conventional career, he would have ended up as boss of a large corporation, such was his talent for business and management. Unlike many of his mobster colleagues, he was level-headed, rational and extremely intelligent, never letting his passions dictate his actions. Throughout most of his career, he managed to evade the law, only serving a short time in prison towards the end of it, and died a rich old man in Florida in 1983. He left behind a fortune of over four hundred million dollars.

Lansky was born Majer Suchowlinski in Grodno, Poland, in 1902. His parents were Jewish, and while he was still a boy, the family emigrated to the United States. They Americanized their name to Lansky, settling in New York, where ten-year-old Meyer, as he was now called, was captivated by the vibrant street life of the city. However, as a small, foreign boy in a rough neighbourhood he quickly had to develop survival skills, and became tough. While he was in school, he came up against the Sicilian street gang led by Lucky Luciano who demanded protection money from him. Lansky refused to pay and, although he was much smaller in stature than his opponents, put up a spirited fight. Luciano was impressed, and the pair became firm friends.

Throughout most of his career, he managed to evade the law, only serving a short time in prison towards the end of it, and died a rich old man in Florida in 1983. He left behind a fortune of over four hundred million dollars.

With an ill-gotten fortune of over four hundred million dollars, Lansky certainly had something to smile about

The brains and the brawn

Growing up in a tough area of Brooklyn, Lansky soon realized that the only way to make big money was to become involved in the various street enterprises that he saw around him. His hard-working father, a garment presser in the clothing industry, had sunk into depression as a result of his family's poverty, and Meyer had no intention of following the same path. He began to join in street gambling games and, with his good head for figures, he often won, hiding his increasingly large bankroll of money in a hole in his mattress. At fifteen, he left school, and his father found him a job as an apprentice tool-maker. However, the job did not last long; by this time, he was becoming involved in all sorts of unsavoury street scams. In 1920, the Volstead Act had brought in Prohibition, providing a new opening for young men like Lansky in buying and selling illegal liquor. The following year, Lansky quit his job and never looked back.

He hooked up with a friend, 'Bugsy' Siegel, and together the pair formed a notorious gang that took on anything from protection rackets to car-jacking and armed robbery. They then moved on to work for Arnold Rothstein, the 'Mr Big' of New York crime, bootlegging scotch and running gambling houses and brothels. Lansky and Siegel were like chalk and cheese: where Lansky always tried to figure out the most effective way to handle a situation, Siegel was hotheaded and trigger-happy to the point of being psychotic. Despite their differences, the two of them were very close, and many believed that Lansky was the only person who could control Siegel's violent streak. In turn, Siegel offered Lansky the protection he needed to pursue his various illegal business activities, and many times saved his friend's life. As a business team, the pair were formidable: Lansky was the brains, and Siegel the brawn, and the partnership lasted for many years until Siegel's reckless behaviour finally got the better of him.

Betraying Bugsy

Along with Siegel, Lansky joined up with his old sparring partner Charles Luciano to become part of the notorious New York mobsters, the Five Points Gang. Early in his career, Lansky helped Luciano bump off Mafia bosses Joe Masseria and Salvatore Maranzano, although as a Jew he was forced to take a back seat in the conflict between the Italian overlords. Luciano then took over 'The Firm', as he called it, and partly because of his close relationship with Lansky, threw the field open to Jewish and other ethnic groups, instead of limiting it to those of Sicilian origin, as his previous bosses had done. His equal opportunities policy was highly successful, and soon the Italian and Jewish gangs were operating an international crime network that boasted all kinds of criminal activities, from gambling and prostitution to drug smuggling and extortion.

By the 1930s, Lansky was a very rich man, despite the fact that Prohibition had now come to an end. He was involved in running illegal casinos across the country, known as 'carpet joints', and had evolved a complex system of paying off politicians to allow him to do so. He then expanded the operation to Cuba. Meanwhile, his old friend and partner, Bugsy Siegel, was in charge of building projects in Las Vegas. However, Siegel was no businessman and had begun to overrun building and decorating costs by millions of dollars. Luciano and other members of the syndicate were convinced that Siegel and his girlfriend, Virginia Hill, were skimming money, and threatened to have Siegel killed. Lansky pleaded for mercy for his friend, and asked for more time so that the casino could turn a profit. Eventually, it did, but by that time it was too late: Siegel was brutally gunned down in his apartment in Beverly Hills. Lansky always claimed that he knew nothing about the killing, but it may have been the case that he was forced to order it.

The final years

Lansky continued to run the syndicate until late in life, expanding into legal areas of business such as investment into hotels and golf courses. In his later years, he was accused of tax evasion, and decided to retire to Israel. However, Israel was not prepared to take a mob boss wanted by the FBI, so he eventually returned to Florida where he was arrested and charged. He served a short prison sentence. Afterwards, he settled in Florida and died of lung cancer in 1983. Thus ended the career of Meyer Lansky, a man who had never sought the limelight, or attracted a great deal of media attention, yet who was one of the most important Mafia godfathers of the twentieth century.

Dutch Schultz

Born in a different time and place, Dutch Schultz was one of those men who might have aspired to greatness. He had brains and vision, plus a definite streak of ruthlessness. However, as he was born into grinding poverty in the Bronx at the beginning of the twentieth century, it is not altogether surprising that he put these attributes to work in the services of organized crime.

Beer Baron of the Bronx

Like many other mobsters of his generation – from Al Capone to Lucky Luciano to Meyer Lansky – it was Prohibition that made Schultz his fortune. Known for a time as 'The Beer Baron of the Bronx', Schultz became one of the most powerful and feared men in New York, before his violent life finally led to a violent death.

Dutch Schultz was born Arthur Simon Flegenheimer on 6 August 1902 in the Bronx, New York. His parents were both German Jews and his mother Emma, in particular, tried to pass religious values on to her son. She was successful only to a limited extent. Schulz did take an interest in religion, but not a consistent one. He described himself at various times as Jewish, Protestant and Catholic. As he grew up, he joined one of the street gangs that ruled the streets of the Bronx. When Schultz was fourteen, his father abandoned the family, and young Arthur decided to adopt the criminal life. He started doing jobs for a local mobster, Marcel

Although he had the face of an 'ordinary Joe', mobster Dutch Schultz was anything but

Poffo. In 1919, when he was seventeen, he was caught burgling an apartment and received his one and only prison sentence.

As often happens, prison only served to turn the young Arthur from apprentice hoodlum to fully fledged criminal. When he came out he had a new name, 'Dutch' Schultz, and a reputation as a hard man. Prohibition had come in the previous year and it was becoming clear that there was big money to be made now that alcohol was illegal. Schultz worked his way up, starting as a hired muscle protecting deliveries, then driving a beer truck, then working in a speakeasy run by a gangster named Joey Noe, a childhood friend. Noe saw Schultz's potential and made him a partner in their bootlegging business. The duo bought their own delivery trucks and gradually forced all the other speakeasy owners in the Bronx to buy their beer from them. Anyone who refused was treated with extreme brutality.

War in gangland

Once they had taken over the business in the Bronx, they turned their attention to Manhattan and stated delivering to speakeasies across the Upper East Side. This soon brought the gang into conflict with 'Legs' Diamond, the mobster who dominated the Manhattan scene. On 15 October 1928, Diamond's men ambushed Joey Noe outside the Chateau Madrid nightclub, shooting him dead. War had been declared; mob money man Arnold Rothstein was shot dead two weeks later. Schultz's main gunman, Bo Weinberg, eventually shot Diamond dead, but not for another three years.

The next threat to Schultz came from within his own organization. In 1931, a gunman named Vincent Coll set himself up as a rival. Angry over an unpaid loan, Schultz brought matters to a head by assassinating Coll's brother. Coll responded by killing four of Schultz's men and hijacking his beer lorries. Schultz refused to stand for this and, after several near misses, he finally had Coll shot dead in a drugstore in February 1932.

Easing in on the numbers racket

By now it was clear that the great Prohibition experiment was coming to an end. Schultz was smart enough to look for another lucrative scam. His attention alighted on the numbers racket, a popular form of gambling particularly prevalent in New York's black communities. Organized crime had paid little attention to the numbers because the individual stakes were generally very small. Schultz, however, realized that if all the different small-scale outfits could be brought together, the total daily take would actually be sizable. With a characteristic mixture of diplomacy and ruthless violence, Schultz proceeded to take over the Harlem lottery.

Soon afterwards, Schultz alighted on another scheme: systematically intimidating the restaurants of New York into paying a weekly amount of protection money – disguised as voluntary membership dues paid to a front organization called the Metropolitan Restaurant & Cafeteria Owners Association. This was run for Schulz by a hood named Jules Martin. Schultz appeared to be riding higher than ever as Prohibition drew to a close, helped by his links to the city's corrupt mayor.

There was more than just a fly in his soup when Dutch was killed – by order of the Mob – in a Newark chop house

The duo bought their own delivery trucks and gradually forced all the other speakeasy owners in the Bronx to buy their beer from them. Anyone who refused was treated with extreme brutality.

The law closes in

Nemesis, however, was just around the corner in the shape of Special Prosecutor Thomas E. Dewey, who was determined to nail Schultz. His chosen weapon was the one that had been so effective against Al Capone in Chicago: tax evasion charges. Rather than catch a gangster red-handed, all the prosecution needed to do was prove that he had substantial earnings and that he had paid no taxes.

Thus, on 25 January 1933, Dutch Schulz was indicted for tax evasion. His immediate response was to go on the run. For more than a year, he avoided the law and carried on running his businesses. Finally, however, he grew tired of running and, in November 1934, he gave himself up for trial.

While out on bail, Schultz discovered that Jules Martin had been skimming money from the restaurant shakedowns. Schultz invited his own lawyer and Martin to a meeting. When Martin admitted skimming, Schultz shocked the lawyer by immediately shooting Martin in the head, killing him instantly.

Violent death

Soon after this incident, Schultz's trial began. The first jury was unable to come to an agreement. A retrial was ordered and, much to Dewey's fury, the jury this time acquitted Schulz. When Dewey started preparing new charges. Schultz decided to put out a hit on Dewey. Fellow mob bosses, including Lucky Luciano, got wind of this and decided it would be very bad for business to have Dewey murdered. Instead, they put out their own hit on Schultz and, on 23 October 1935, Schultz and three of his men were shot dead in the Palace Chop House in Newark, New Jersey. Thus ended the career of one of the mob's most formidable gangsters.

Arnold Rothstein

Arnold 'The Brain' Rothstein masterminded the transformation of the New York criminal underworld into a series of highly efficient organized crime syndicates, operating gambling, prostitution, bootlegging and narcotics operations on a grand scale. He is remembered today for his alleged involvement in the Black Sox scandal of 1919, in which it was rumoured that the Chicago baseball team was paid to lose an important match in the World Series. However, his involvement was never verified. He finally met his end in 1928, when he was shot, apparently in a drunken brawl, after failing to pay a gambling debt. Although Rothstein was not a violent man, his business dealings brought him into close contact with many cold-blooded killers, and it was his connections with these men that ultimately brought about his demise.

'The Big Bankroll'

Rothstein was the son of a wealthy New York Jewish businessman, Abraham Rothstein. As a child, he felt unloved by his parents, and was extremely jealous of his older brother Harry, whom he felt they preferred. Arnold did not do well at school, though he showed a talent for mathematics, and dropped out aged sixteen. While Harry chose to become a rabbi, Arnold began a career as a travelling salesman. Then tragedy struck: Harry contracted pneumonia and died. The effect on Arnold was to make him feel guilty for his past jealousy of his brother, and somehow responsible for his death. He attempted to improve family relations by returning home, working in his father's factory and resuming his religious faith, but his father continued to reject him, so he gave up trying to please his parents and moved on.

Rothstein now began to use his mathematical skills in the pursuit of gambling. He started to play pool, poker and craps for money. He also bet on boxing fights, elections, baseball games and horse races. In addition, he booked bets for other people and lent money at high interest rates. In order to impress his colleagues and customers, he began to carry a large wad of money around with him, thus earning the nickname 'The Big Bankroll'. He soon gained a reputation as a cautious, intelligent gambler and began to make

Rothstein is credited with consolidating organized crime into what later became known as the Mafia.

Rothstein – relying on his brains rather than hired brawn, he was a particularly successful, 'white-collar' criminal mastermind

a lot of money, which he invested in legitimate businesses such as shops and car dealerships.

A life of luxury

One of those whom Rothstein impressed was Carolyn Greene, a young actress. When the couple decided to marry, Rothstein took her home to meet his parents. Abraham asked Carolyn if she would change her faith to become Jewish but she refused. As a result, the Rothstein parents stayed away from the couple's wedding; apparently, when Abraham heard news of it, he recited the Jewish prayer of the dead, the Kaddish, for his son.

The newly married Arnold promised his wife that he would earn as much money as he could to keep her in luxury. She knew of her husband's gambling interests, but later claimed not to have discussed any details of them with him. Over the next few years, Rothstein set up several gambling clubs, enhancing his reputation as one of the best pool players in the city. The clubs attracted wealthy customers who pitted their skills against Rothstein's, both at pool and at cards. As well as running the clubs, Rothstein conducted his many other business ventures from his 'office' at Lindy's Restaurant on the corner of Broadway and 49th Street, often standing on the street outside to collect money, surrounded by his bodyguards.

Godfather of the Mafia

By 1913, Rothstein had become one of the most powerful figures in New York, with friends in high places as well as low. His polite manner, his formidable intelligence and, of course, his tolerance towards all kinds of immoral activities made him a central conduit between the corrupt politicians of Tammany Hall and the ruthless mobsters of the criminal world. On the one hand, he received protection from Tammany Hall boss Charles F. Murphy and his advisor Tom Foley; on the other, he was in league with mob bosses such as Lucky Luciano, Meyer Lansky and Bugsy Siegel. Such was his standing in the crime world that he became known by many nicknames, including 'The Brain', 'The Fixer' and 'Mr Big'. As well as his gambling interests, he ran a real estate enterprise, a bail bond business and a racing stables. He amassed a fortune, and expanded his interests in and around the New York area. Today, Rothstein is credited with consolidating organized crime into what later became known as the Mafia.

As well as betting on horse races and baseball games, Rothstein was also rumoured to 'fix' them. The most sensational of these rumours hit the headlines in 1919, during the World Series, when members of the Chicago White Sox team agreed to lose the game to the Cincinnati team for payment. In 1921, eight of the men were convicted of fraud and were banned from playing baseball again professionally. Rothstein was also called to testify in the case, but was acquitted due to lack of evidence. To this day, it is still unclear exactly what his involvement was in the scandal.

The day of reckoning

Despite his links with the criminal underworld, Rothstein always seemed to keep his hands clean and emerge unscathed from any scandal. Up until the day of his death, he was never convicted of any criminal activity. However, in 1928, his luck ran out. He took part in a high-stakes game of poker that lasted several days. In the end, he lost a total of over three hundred thousand dollars and, in the weeks that ensued, did not pay off his debts. The host of the game, George McManus, eventually called him to a meeting in a hotel room to settle the matter. Rothstein was then somehow shot in the abdomen. McManus was arrested but later acquitted due to lack of evidence. The shot proved fatal when Rothstein died several days later. Thus, the kingpin of the New York underworld was finally brought down by a dispute over a game of cards.

Bugsy Siegel

One of the most contradictory of criminals, Bugsy Siegel was, on the one hand a notoriously violent gangster, always ready to shoot first and think later (his nickname 'Bugsy' came from his apparent tendency to go 'bugs' with rage) whilst on the other, he was a smooth charmer who became the Mafia's front man, first in Hollywood and later in Las Vegas.

Out of the ghetto

Bugsy Siegel was born Benjamin Siegelbaum in 1905. His parents were Russian Jewish immigrants who lived in Williamsburg, Brooklyn, one of several city neighbourhoods to be dubbed 'Hell's Kitchen'. Benjamin soon saw crime as the most likely way out of this teeming ghetto. By the age of twelve, he was running a protection racket along with his friend Moey Sedway. Not long after, he met another young would-be gangster, and this time the meeting changed his life. The youth in question was named Meyer Lansky and the two formed a natural partnership. Lansky was the brains, Siegel the brawn. Both were utterly ruthless.

Lansky and Siegel formed a gang and gained a local reputation. Lansky then became friendly with another local gang leader, Charlie 'Lucky' Luciano. This was unusual, as generally the Italian gangs refused to have anything to do with the Jewish gangs. Luciano, however, clearly recognized true criminal talent when he saw it and refused to break his relationship with Lansky and Siegel. The friendship was confirmed when Luciano was sent to jail on drugs charges, after a policeman's son had given evidence against him. On Luciano's release from prison, Lansky and Siegel told him to leave town for the night and make sure he had an alibi. Sure enough, that night the policeman's son disappeared, never to be seen again.

Murder and mayhem

By now Prohibition had come into force, following the Volstead Act of 1919, and organized crime was developing as a result. Suddenly, the general public wanted something – alcohol – that they could only get from criminals. Siegel and Lansky took to bootlegging with relish, both manufacturing rotgut whisky themselves and hijacking lorry loads of booze from other gangsters. These activities brought them to the attention of the Mafia's overall leader, Joe 'The Boss' Masseria. A power struggle ensued. Charlie

Six foot tall and good looking, Siegel was perfect for Hollywood: a real gangster who looked like a movie star.

Bugsy Siegel with movie heart-throb George Raft at a Hollywood court house, where Siegel was charged with bookmaking

Luciano decided to make a deal with Masseria's great rival, Sal Maranzano, and enlisted a team of hit men, including Siegel, to kill Joe Masseria as he had lunch in a Coney Island restaurant. Soon afterwards, Luciano killed Maranzano in turn, and became the top Mafia boss on the east coast.

Unimpressed by this, yet another rival Mafia chief, Waxey Gordon, took out a contract on Siegel and Lansky during 1932. Two of his men, Andy and Louis Frabrazzo, planted a bomb in Siegel's house. However, just before it exploded, Siegel discovered the bomb and threw it out of the window. Slightly injured by the blast, he was taken to hospital where he remained for several days, leaving only to track down another Frabrazzo brother, Tony, whom he murdered in front of his elderly parents. Siegel was then driven back to the hospital, where he climbed back through the window unnoticed.

High society

This escapade brought serious police attention down on Siegel, forcing him to lay low for a while. Meanwhile, he was beginning to get impatient with his role as Lansky's number two. Lansky clearly sensed this and, rather than test the limits of their friendship, or end up as yet another victim of Siegel's deadly temper, sent him out west in 1936 to run the California branch of the mob.

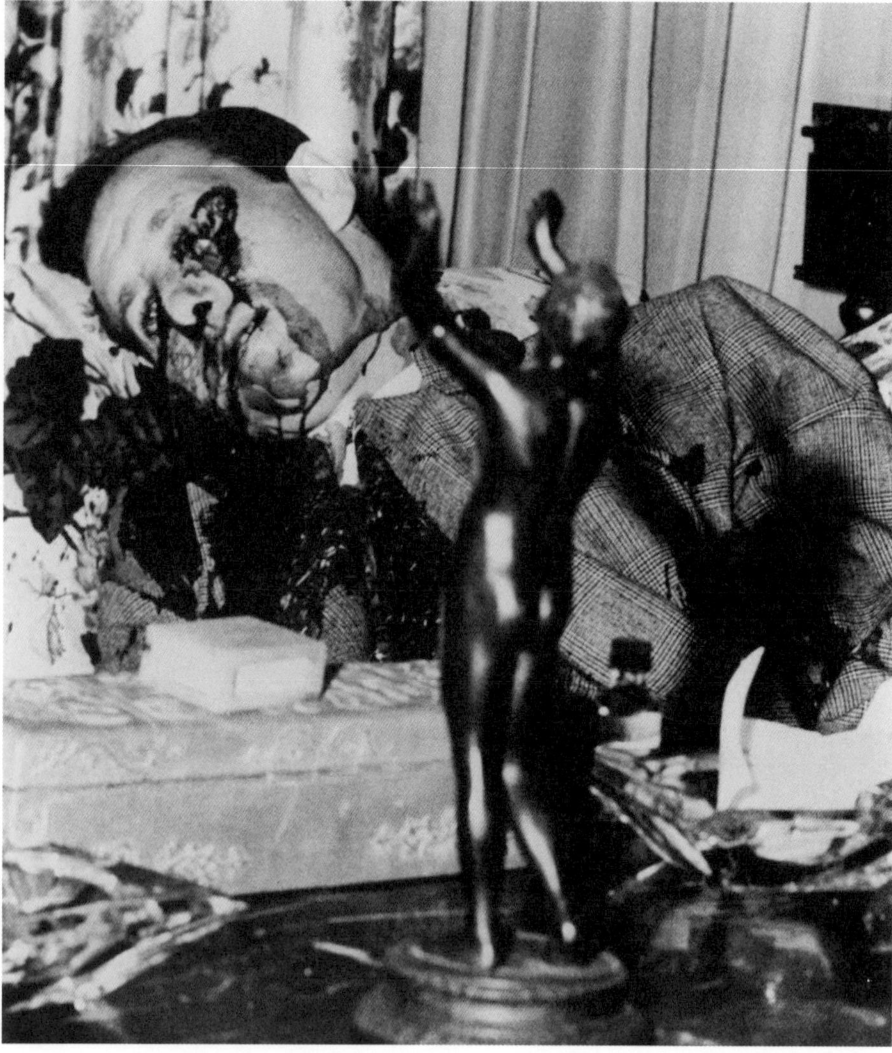

Bugsy's death was, fittingly, like a scene from the Hollywood movies; a world that had opened its arms to the debonair mobster

The only problem was that the west coast mob already had a leader, Jack Dragna, notionally the head of the Italian Protective League. After initial friction, Dragna kept on running the gambling rackets, while Siegel concentrated on running the corrupt unions that controlled much of what went on in Hollywood. Siegel's arrival in Hollywood allowed him to see his old friend George Raft, an actor whose expertise at playing gangsters stemmed from his own experience of growing up among them. Raft was Siegel's entry into Hollywood high society, and he soon became the archetypal player, with a string of mistresses. Six foot tall and good looking, Siegel was perfect for Hollywood: a real gangster who looked like a movie star.

By the mid-1940s, just after the Second World War, Siegel was getting restless, so Lansky had another idea. Why didn't the mob set up a casino in Nevada, a state that had legalized gambling? Siegel was not sure at first: after all, at the time Nevada was little more than an expanse of scrubby desert. However, after going out there to investigate further, Siegel discovered that there were already some gambling operations in a town called Las Vegas. Soon he had a plan.

The biggest casino in the world

Siegel decided to build the biggest, smartest hotel and casino operation there had ever been in Las Vegas. It was to be called the Flamingo. He raised a million dollars from a mixture of fellow

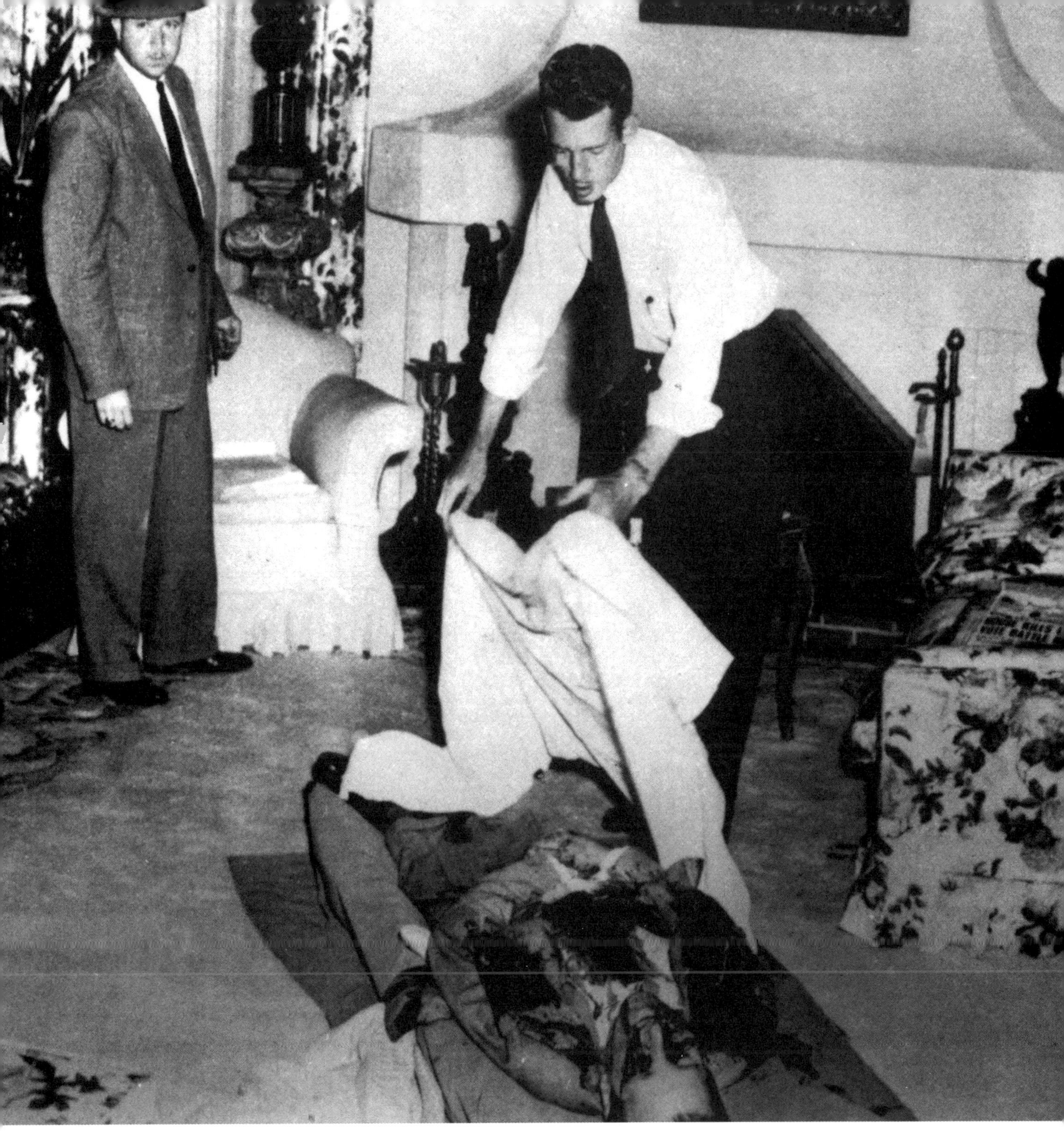

mobsters and Hollywood contacts. The costs spiralled to six million dollars and Siegel's investors grew worried. The Flamingo finally opened just before Christmas 1946. It was a disaster: the initial earnings were pitiful. A meeting of mobsters was convened, all of them ready to demand Siegel's head. Lansky persuaded them to wait six months. Remarkably enough, Siegel managed to turn things around. By the end of May the casino was making a profit. Perhaps it was not enough, or perhaps his fellow mobsters simply thought that Siegel needed to be taught a lesson. Either way, in June 1947 Bugsy Siegel, veteran of dozens of hits, was finally the victim of one. Two men burst into his Hollywood apartment and shot him dead.

Used to clearing up the mess Bugsy caused in life, the police had the grisly task of clearing up the gangster himself in death

Tellingly, none of his former associates came to his funeral, not even Meyer Lansky.

Mickey Cohen

Mickey Cohen, like his mentor Bugsy Siegel, was a strange mixture of charm and menace. Together these two men, both New York Jews from poverty-stricken backgrounds, carved out a place for organised crime in Hollywood. Unlike Siegel, Mickey Cohen survived well enough in the Mafia jungle to make it past sixty years old, and to die in his own bed, two rare achievements in the underworld of crime.

Moonshine madness

Meyer Harris 'Mickey' Cohen was born in New York City on 4 September 1913. He spent his early years in the sprawling slum that was Brownsville, Brooklyn, before his family moved out west to Boyle Heights, Los Angeles when he was six years old. His family ran a drugstore there, in the midst of what was a largely Orthodox Jewish neighbourhood. This was during the years immediately following Prohibition, and the drugstore soon became a front for a moonshine liquor operation. By age nine young Mickey was happily involved in this family business, and was arrested making a delivery of his brother's moonshine. His brother, however, had enough local connections for the police to let Mickey go. Mickey had had his first taste for the gangster lifestyle and he liked it.

Fighting and gambling

Another thing he liked was boxing. Though small of stature, Mickey Cohen had plenty of aggression and power. He fought as a featherweight and won an amateur championship, aged fifteen. At that point he left home, determined to turn pro. He headed for New York where his boxing reputation grew and - the sport being a big favourite with mobsters - he made the acquaintance of a number of leading figures in organised crime, including Owney Madden, the man behind such mob-run operations as the Cotton Club and the Mafia's very own resort in Hot Springs, Arkansas.

Mickey Cohen's fight career peaked with a bout against the featherweight World Champion, Tommy Paul. This resulted in a bad beating for

Mickey Cohen (right) next to his right-hand man, Johnny Stompanato, during a trial in 1950. Stompanato was murdered eight years later by Hollywood actress Lana Turner's fourteen-year-old daughter

Cohen, and he promptly quit boxing. He moved straight back into crime. He started by holding up gambling joints. This was a risky business, as many of the places were run by the mob. Cohen was lucky that, rather than kill him, the local mob realised Cohen had a talent they could use. He moved from New York to Cleveland to Chicago, graduating from holding up card games to running them. Along the way he gained the personal approval of top Chicago boss Al Capone.

When things got a little too hot in Chicago, Cohen moved back to Cleveland for a while, working with Lou Rothkopf. Cleveland didn't have enough action for Cohen, so Rothkopf suggested Mickey take a trip to California where his associates Meyer Lansky and Bugsy Siegel were staking out their turf in Hollywood.

Mickey took the advice and made his way up the ranks of the organization to become Siegel's right-hand man. He was soon embroiled in fighting between the Siegel and Lansky outfit and a rival outfit, led by Jack Dragna, the previous LA mob boss. This was a conflict between old and new, Italian and Jewish. The conflict frequently became bloody, and Mickey Cohen was lucky to escape unscathed from several attempts on his life. Once, members of Dragna's gang opened up with machine guns as Cohen sat in his car. Ducking down, he managed to drive his car to safety, shaking off his pursuers.

Hollywood beckons

Increasingly, Siegel's attention became taken up with establishing a giant casino, The Flamingo, in Las Vegas. Siegel was the front man for this project, but when the Flamingo made an initial huge loss, he was suspected of skimming off money from the project and his fellow mobsters ordered his death. The hit was carried out with clinical efficiency in 1947. Mickey Cohen must have suspected he would be tainted by his boss' misdeeds but instead he was promoted to become the number one boss on the West Coast.

Now Cohen started to move in elevated circles. He became friendly with Harry Cohn, boss of Columbia Pictures and assorted movie stars, including Frank Sinatra and Sammy Davis Jr. At one stage he was caught in a dispute between two of his friends. Cohn was furious that the black Sammy Davis Jr should have an open affair with white actress Kim Novak, and wanted Mickey Cohen to have Davis killed. Cohen managed to talk him out of it.

Mickey's right-hand man, the notorious gunman Johnny Stompanato, also got involved with the Hollywood elite. He had affairs with Ava Gardner and then Lana Turner. This relationship led to a scandal when Lana Turner's fourteen-year-old daughter, Cheryl Crane, shot Stompanato dead on 4 April 1958.

Life in Alcatraz

The scandal once again drew unwanted publicity towards Cohen. Matters got worse following the 1960 election of John F. Kennedy. His brother Robert Kennedy became Attorney General and was determined to stamp out Mafia activity. Soon Cohen was arrested for tax evasion for the second time in his life (he had already served a brief sentence in the early 1950s). This time he was looking at a much longer sentence, but given the chance to walk free if he informed on other major organised crime figures.

Cohen refused and was sentenced to fifteen years in prison. He spent the first part of his sentence in the notorious Alcatraz prison and, when he was finally released in the early 1970s, went into semi-retirement. He wrote a book, *In My Own Words*, about his criminal career. However, it was not long before he succumbed to the ravages of stomach cancer. He died on 29 July 1976 at home in California.

Members of Dragna's gang opened up with machine guns as Cohen sat in his car. He managed to duck down and drive his car to safety.

Erminia Giuliano

Erminia Giuliano is one of a new breed of women who head the Mafia families of Sicily. She breaks the traditional stereotype of the Italian wife and mother as a docile homemaker who leaves the business side of things to the men. Like other female Mafia bosses, Giuliano came into a position of power because so many of her male relatives had been killed in feuds between the warring Mafia families. And once she was there, she proved as strong a force – if not stronger – than her male counterparts.

Giuliano came to prominence as head of the Comorra, the loosely connected group of Mafia families operating in and around Naples. The Italian police viewed her as one of Italy's most dangerous criminals, and ranked her among the country's top thirty most wanted. Neapolitan police chief Carlo Gualdi regarded her as 'a true leader' and said that she had the ruthless qualities associated with the male Mafia Godfathers of the past. In fact, the Queen of the Clan, as she became known, sometimes seemed more bloodthirsty than her male relatives.

Glamorous mugshot – Erminia Giuliano insisted on having time to change and do her make up before she was taken down to the police station for questioning

Fake leopard-skin glamour

Giuliano became boss after her brothers were arrested and jailed. One by one, brothers Luigi 'O Re' ('The King'), Carmine, Raffaele, Guglielmo, and Salvatore, had been incarcerated for a variety of crimes, mostly connected to the running of their illegal gambling operations. Also wanted by the police, Erminia went on the run for ten months and was finally discovered hiding in her daughter's home, behind a secret trap door under the kitchen. She made headlines by refusing to be escorted to Pozzuoli jail before taking a shower and changing. A beautician was called to the house to do her make up, and she had her hair done. She then donned a fake leopard-skin outfit and, suitably attired for media attention, then agreed to leave. Erminia was determined, even when arrested, to live up to her nickname, Celeste – 'heavenly'.

Erminia is not the only 'Godmother', or 'Madrina', as these female heads of the family have become known, among the Mafia families. Others include Maria and Teresa Zappia, who led

the Ndrangheta, a Calabrian crime syndicate; Concetta Scalisi, who took power after her well-known father Giuseppe and brother Salvatore were gunned down; and Pupetta ('Little Doll') Maresca. Maresca's husband was murdered while she was still a teenager, and she got her revenge by murdering the killer. So violent was Maresca that, when she was jailed, four prison officers were detailed to guard her at all times.

The women shoot it out

Another notorious Godmother was Marisa Merico, whose father was a Mafia boss and whose mother came from Blackpool, England. Marisa grew up in England after her parents split up and her mother returned there, but kept in touch with her Italian relatives and later headed a money-laundering operation. Also well-known in Italy was Maria Licciardi, called 'The Princess', who hit the headlines as a Mafia boss when war broke out between her family and that of Giuliano. The fighting between the two clans resulted in the deaths of fifty family members in 2000.

The new, female-oriented style of Mafia killing is illustrated by an episode that took place in 2002 in the small mountain town of Lauro near Naples. Here, rivalry broke out between the Cava and Graziano families, who both belong to the Neapolitan Mafia, the Camorra. In a deadly shoot-out, three people were killed, and five injured. But the victims, and some of the perpetrators, were not the macho gangsters that one would expect to commit such crimes. They were women.

The youngest of the victims was Clarrisa Cava, a sixteen-year-old schoolgirl. The other two were her aunts, Michelina Cava and Maria Scibelli, who had attempted to protect their niece by throwing themselves in front of her. Two other young family members were seriously injured: Clarissa's sister Felicia and her cousin Italia. After the shoot-out, the police arrested nine members of the Graziano family for the murders. The suspects included four women: Alba Scibelli, her mother-in-law Chiara Manzi, and her two daughters, Stefania and Chiara.

A culture of violence

Clearly, the code of honour within the Mafia had changed. Now, not only were women directing operations, they were also involved in the actual killings – a role which, until recently, had been left to the men to carry out. At the time of the shoot-out, numerous commentators voiced their fears that an escalation in Mafia violence would take place now that women were also involved in the violence.

On a more positive note, there is some evidence that the increasingly powerful role of women in the Mafia may also be changing the culture for the better. In some cases, Mafia women have turned informer, informing on their husbands and brothers to the police when gang warfare has threatened the future of their children. In the same way, women have sometimes sought to escape from violent marriages by turning in their menfolk, knowing that they and their children will not be safe until the male members of the family are locked up. However, despite these encouraging signs, to date the Godmothers have not succeeded in reversing the violent culture of revenge killings in the Camorra, which continue to blight the lives not only of Mafia families, but of the ordinary people caught up in the crossfire.

History of crime: a Camorra (the Neapolitan Mafia) trial in Viterbo, 1911. The larger cage contained thirty-four of the accused; the smaller, the informer

AUDACIOUS OUTLAWS

From Wild West heroes Butch Cassidy and the Sundance Kid to Ned Kelly, folk hero of the Australian bush, those on the run from the law have provided a colourful cast of legendary historical characters to entertain us. The names of Bonnie and Clyde, John Dillinger and Charles Arthur 'Pretty Boy' Floyd, as well as those of Cassidy and Kelly, have a modern-day romance about them that has continued to fascinate new generations of readers and film-goers. Their romantic aura derives in part from the times they lived in – times of danger and excitement that contrast with the safer lives we lead today. It is also to do with the admiration we feel for those courageous enough to break away from the conventions of ordinary life.

In part, their stories are also the stuff of legend, as outlaws are idealized as apparent Robin Hood figures, robbing the rich to feed the poor. In some cases, the Robin Hood image has some justification: for example, Pretty Boy Floyd made a point of destroying mortgage documents during his bank robberies, a move that made him very popular during the Depression years when banks were constantly foreclosing on poor farmers. In other cases, the reality of the outlaw's life was actually sordid and gruesome: for example, Clyde Barrow of Bonnie and Clyde fame was in fact a brutally violent man. Whatever the reality, however, it is the outlaws' spirit of adventure, the thrill they gave the public as their devil-may-care recklessness was followed escapade by escapade by the press of the day, and their refusal to conform to the conventions of society that lend them an enduring appeal.

Butch Cassidy and the Sundance Kid

Butch Cassidy and the Sundance Kid were among the last of a dying breed of outlaws and migrant cowboys in the Wild West at the turn of the twentieth century. Along with their flamboyant gang, the Wild Bunch, they stole horses, robbed banks and trains, and generally lived outside the law. Eventually, as the authorities closed in on them, they decamped to South America, going straight but then continuing their life of crime and excitement until they met their end. After their death, they became legendary folk heroes, and were immortalized in the 1969 film *Butch Cassidy and the Sundance Kid.*

Butch Cassidy – as stylish an outlaw as they came

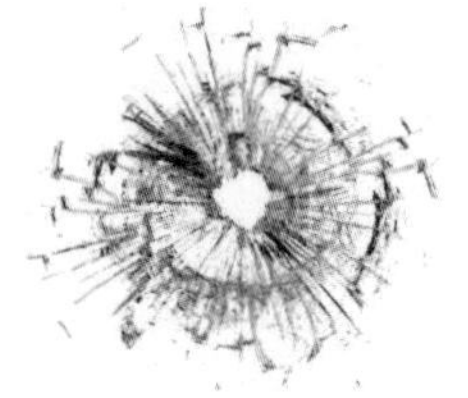

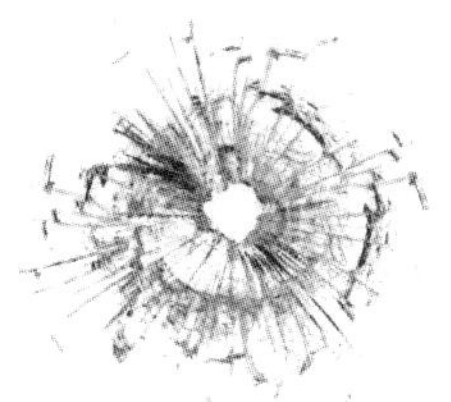

Butch Cassidy was born Robert Leroy Parker in 1866. He grew up on a ranch near Circleville, Utah, where his parents were Mormons. As a boy, he once stole a horse, under the influence of an old cattle rustler called Mike Cassidy – from whom he later derived his last name. Life on the strictly-run family ranch proved too dull for young Robert and, before long, he left home to become a migrant cowboy, working around the country. For a short period, he also worked as a butcher, which is where it is thought he got his nickname 'Butch' from.

Fearless adventurers

Cassidy soon tired of trying to make an honest living, and began to steal cattle. He was caught and imprisoned in a Wyoming jail for two years. When he came out, he started to live the life of an outlaw in earnest. He was well suited to it: a quick-witted man with a great deal of charm, he was also a fearless adventurer who could always come up with an audacious plan to get himself out of a tight corner. Such was his charisma that he soon gathered a gang of notorious desperadoes around him, who became known as the Wild Bunch.

His future partner in crime, Harry Alonzo Longabaugh, was born in Philadelphia, Pennsylvania, the youngest of five children. His parents were poor but had a strong religious faith. As a young man, Harry left home and travelled around the country seeking employment. In 1887, broke and out of work, he stole a horse in Sundance, Wyoming. He was caught and served an eighteen-month sentence in the Sundance town jail. The name of the town gave him his nickname from that time on: the Sundance Kid.

The Sundance Kid and his wife, Etta Place. She was rumoured to have been Butch Cassidy's lover too, but the exact relationships between the three remain unclear

Soon after the pair met up, Sundance became Cassidy's right-hand man. They developed a strong partnership that lasted through thick and thin, until their deaths many years later. Ben 'The Tall Texan' Kirkpatrick was another gang member, known as a lady killer; others included Bill Tod Carver, 'Deaf Charlie' Hanks, Tom 'Peep'

The Wild Bunch went on to commit the longest sequence of successful robberies in the history of the Wild West.

The Wild Bunch (left to right): (standing) Bill Carver, Harvey 'Kid Curry' Logan; (sitting) Harry 'Sundance Kid' Longabaugh, Ben 'Tall Texan' Kirkpatrick and Butch Cassidy

O'Day and 'Wat the Watcher' Punteney. Perhaps the most infamous of all was Harvey Logan, alias Kid Curry, who joined the Wild Bunch after committing a string of robberies with his own gang. Curry was described by William Pinkerton, head of the famous Pinkerton detective agency, as 'the most vicious outlaw in America', and was known to be a cold-blooded killer. Pinkerton wrote: 'He has not one single redeeming feature. He is the only criminal I know of who does not have one single good point.' However, popular reports attest that Curry was actually a quiet, polite fellow who had many friends, and who impressed women with his gentlemanly ways. It seems that he reserved his viciousness for representatives of the law, especially those from Pinkerton's agency.

The Wild Bunch

Several women also rode with the outlaw band. The best known was Etta Place, who married the Sundance Kid and stayed with the gang throughout their adventures. Little is known about her, but it has been suggested that her real name was Ann Bassett, a girl from a ranch in Brown's Park, who at one time had been involved in cattle rustling. Some believe that, as well as being Sundance's wife, she was also Cassidy's girlfriend, but the relationship between the three remains unclear.

The Wild Bunch went on to commit the longest sequence of successful robberies in the history of the Wild West. Their first bank robbery was in Montpelier, Idaho, in 1896. Moving on to Wyoming, they robbed an Overland Flyer train, and, after a shoot-out, got away with thirty thousand dollars. Their next train heist, also in Wyoming, netted them only about fifty dollars, but after that they robbed the bank in Winnemucca, Nevada, and came away with over thirty thousand dollars. The Wild Bunch's last job was in 1901, when they robbed a Northern Pacific train in Montana and stole forty thousand dollars.

Escape to South America

By now, the railroads had hired the Pinkerton Agency to catch the gang, and time was fast running out for them. With Pinkerton's men hot on their heels, they split up. Cassidy and the Sundance Kid, along with Etta Place, headed down to South America. The Tall Texan was caught and imprisoned, and later met his end while robbing a train. Carver and Deaf Charlie were also killed. Kid Curry was imprisoned in Knoxville, Tennessee, until he made a daring escape. Some believe he was later shot during a train robbery, but there is also some evidence that he lived to a ripe old age on a ranch in Patagonia, with a Spanish wife who bore him eight children.

Butch Cassidy, the Sundance Kid and Etta Place bought a ranch in Argentina and lived peacefully for several years before they ran out of money and the men turned to their old ways once more. The pair are thought to have met their end after holding up a payroll transport in the mountains of Bolivia, when they were pursued by troops and apparently killed in a shoot-out. However, there is some disagreement as to what really happened. Some believe that the bandits were not in fact Cassidy and Sundance, but another pair of outlaws. Others maintain that either Cassidy or Sundance, or both of them, committed suicide after being wounded in the shoot-out.

Whatever the truth, the legendary pair went down in American history as the last of the great outlaws of the Wild West. For many, their deaths spelt the end of an era: a time when, at the end of the nineteenth century, the tough, freedom-loving spirit of the pioneers of the Wild West fought long and hard against the greedy profiteering and dreary bureaucracy of the state authorities.

Bonnie and Clyde

Bonnie Parker and Clyde Barrow were among the first celebrity criminals of the twentieth century. During the years of the Great Depression in the 1930s, they shocked America with a series of murders, kidnaps, bank robberies and hold-ups, leaving a trail of devastation wherever they went. The pair are known to have committed at least thirteen murders during their career. Barrow was renowned as a cold-blooded killer, though some allege that Parker herself was not, and that she left her lover to do the dirty work. However, the truth of the matter will probably never be known, because Bonnie and Clyde weren't taken

Publicity-loving Bonnie and Clyde posing with the tools of their trade – guns and a fast getaway car

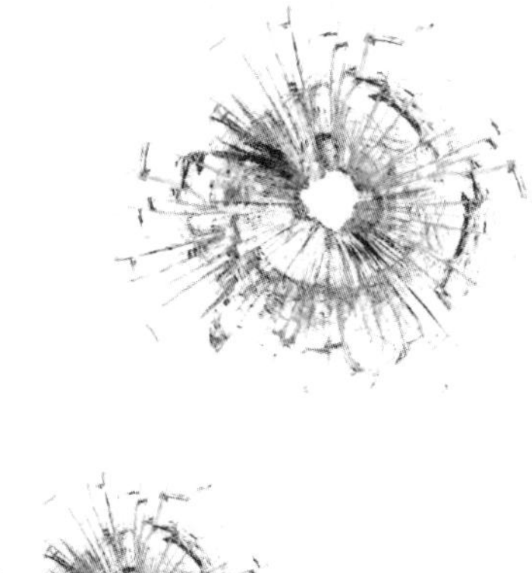

alive. After being hotly pursued by police for several years, they finally died in an ambush when their car was pumped full of bullets.

Bonnie Parker was born in Rowena, Texas, in 1910. At sixteen, she married a man named Ray Thornton. She was madly in love with Thornton and had two intertwined hearts, with their names, tattooed on the inside of her thigh. However, shortly after they were married, Thornton received a long prison sentence for murder. With her husband incarcerated for the foreseeable future, Parker was forced to take a waitressing job and wait for him. She did not wait very long.

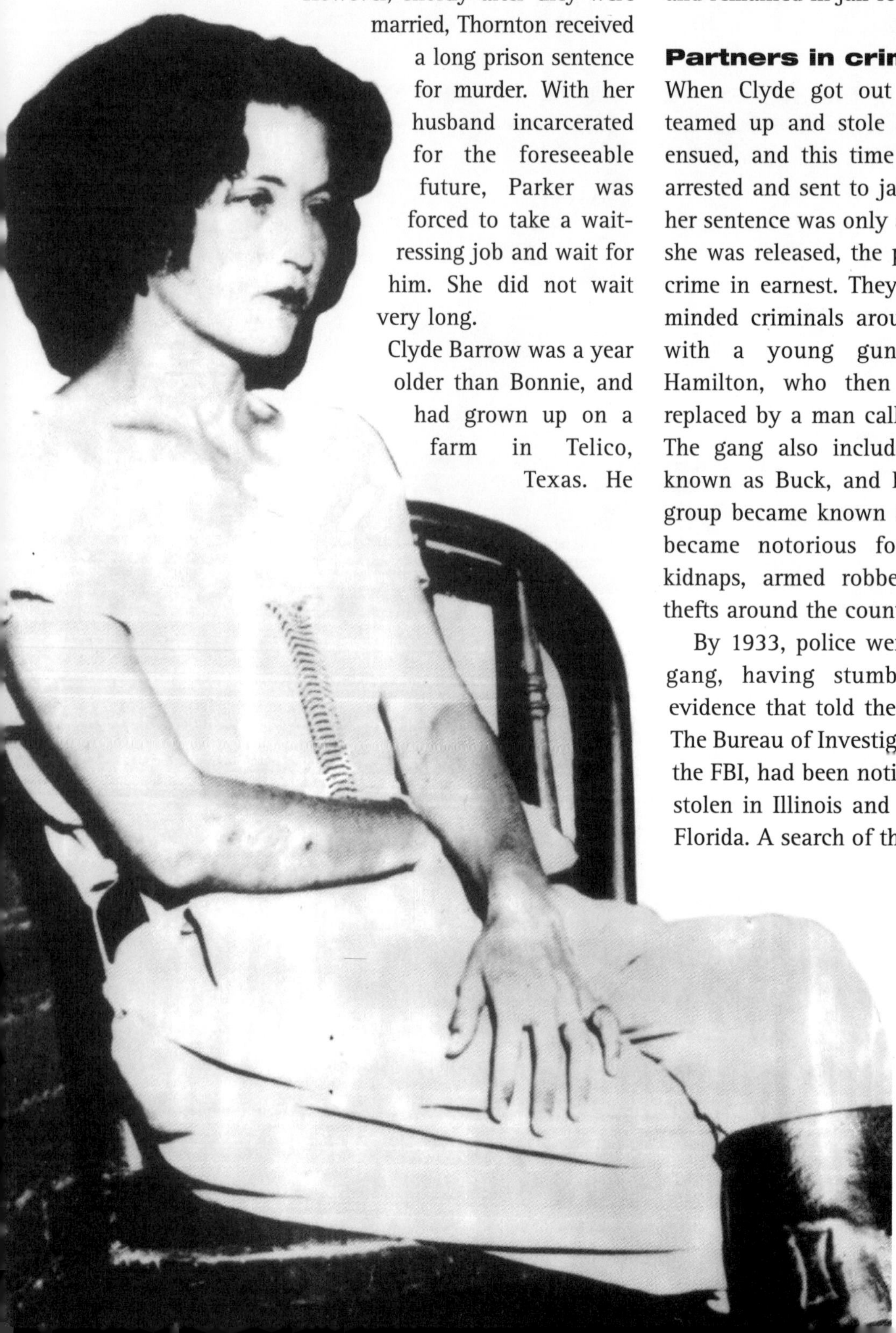

Clyde Barrow was a year older than Bonnie, and had grown up on a farm in Telico, Texas. He was one of many children in a large, poverty-stricken family. In 1926, he was arrested for car theft, but continued his life of crime, committing a string of robberies in the Dallas area. Four years later, by now a hardened criminal, he met Bonnie. However, not long after their meeting, he was jailed. He made an escape, helped by Bonnie, but was apprehended after only a week, and remained in jail for the following two years.

Partners in crime

When Clyde got out of jail, he and Bonnie teamed up and stole a car in Texas. A chase ensued, and this time it was Bonnie who was arrested and sent to jail. Clyde waited for her – her sentence was only a few months – and when she was released, the pair began their career of crime in earnest. They formed a group of like-minded criminals around them, first travelling with a young gunman named Raymond Hamilton, who then dropped out and was replaced by a man called William Daniel Jones. The gang also included Clyde's brother Ivan, known as Buck, and Buck's wife Blanche. The group became known as the Barrow Gang, and became notorious for a series of murders, kidnaps, armed robberies, burglaries and car thefts around the country.

By 1933, police were hot on the trail of the gang, having stumbled across a piece of evidence that told them who the culprits were. The Bureau of Investigation, which later became the FBI, had been notified of a Ford automobile stolen in Illinois and abandoned at Pawhuska, Florida. A search of the car revealed a medicine

A glamorous Bonnie – she had an addiction to bad men and fast living that was to prove her downfall

The group became known as the Barrow Gang, and became notorious for a series of murders, kidnaps, armed robberies, burglaries and car thefts around the country.

bottle and, when special agents called at the drugstore where it was bought, the prescription was found to have been filled in by a relative of Clyde Barrow. After further investigation, it became clear that the occupants of the stolen car had been Bonnie, Clyde and Clyde's brother. A warrant was issued for their arrest, and the hunt began in earnest.

Hunting down the killers

On 29 July 1933, police caught up with the outlaws in Iowa. During the subsequent shoot-out, Buck was killed and Blanche was arrested. A few months later, William Daniel Jones was captured, this time in Houston, Texas. Undeterred, Bonnie and Clyde carried on by themselves. By this time, they were well known to the public. The Barrow Gang's cavalier attitude towards killing their victims had struck fear into the hearts of people, and their crimes had been reported in the most sensational terms in the national press.

Bonnie and Clyde's flamboyant reputation had also been enhanced by various publicity stunts. The Ford Motor Company had advertised their automobiles with a letter signed 'Clyde Champion Barrow', alleged to have been written

Clyde Barrow – a sharp-suited sharp shooter

by the gangster. In it, Barrow praised Ford cars as 'dandy'. In addition, Bonnie had had a poem called 'The Story of Bonnie and Clyde' published in several newspapers, showing her to be quite a talented wordsmith.

On 22 November 1933, the police set a trap for the couple in Grand Prairie, Texas. However, Bonnie and Clyde managed to escape, holding up and stealing a passing car. They later abandoned it in Oklahoma. The following year, in January, they helped five prisoners make a daring escape from a jail in Waldo, Texas. During the escape, two prison guards were shot.

Final ride – the bullet-riddled car of Bonnie and Clyde

Cold-blooded murder

In 1934, the pair hit the headlines once more when they killed two young highway patrolmen in Texas before the officers could reach for their guns. Five days later came the news of another police officer killed in Oklahoma. Not long after, they abducted and wounded a police chief. By this time, the law enforcement authorities were absolutely determined to catch the killers, posting 'wanted' signs all over the country, and distributing the outlaws' photographs, fingerprints and other data to all their officers.

Bonnie and Clyde's days were numbered as soon as they became killers in earnest. In 1934 they shot two highway patrolmen, seemingly in cold blood

The increased efforts to apprehend Bonnie and Clyde paid off, and the trail grew hot when an FBI agent found out that they had been visiting the home of the Methvin family in a remote area of Louisiana. Henry Methvin was one of the prisoners whom Bonnie and Clyde had helped to escape from the Texas jail. Police were tipped off that the pair had held a party in Black

Lake, Louisiana, on 21 May and were due to return two days later.

On the morning of 23 May, a posse of police officers hid in the bushes on the highway near Sailes, Bienville Parish, Lousiana, and managed to ambush the outlaws. In early daylight, the car appeared and, before it could drive away, the police opened fire. They took no chances, and fired round after round of bullets into the car, which became spattered with holes. The couple, who were riding in the front, died instantly.

Despite the fact that Bonnie and Clyde were responsible for more than a dozen murders, and that Clyde was known to be a highly violent man, their glamorous reputation lived on for many years. Several movies were made about their lives, including *You Only Live Once* (1937), *The Bonnie Parker Story* (1958) and – most memorably – *Bonnie and Clyde* (1967), directed by Arthur Penn and starring Warren Beatty and Faye Dunaway. Despite the deaths they caused and the havoc they wreaked in people's lives, their spirited attempt to break away from poverty and live a free life outside the conventions of society continues to hold a romantic appeal for successive generations.

John Dillinger

The bank robber John Dillinger was the original 'Public Enemy Number One', the first man to be branded by the FBI as America's most dangerous criminal. However, while the state regarded him as a menace, there were many who saw him as a hero, a latter-day Robin Hood. This dual status was a result of the times in which he lived. In the early 1930s, America was going through the Depression. Many banks had gone bust, taking people's savings with them. Others were busy foreclosing on small debtors and taking their houses. The public no longer trusted the banking system and when outlaws robbed the banks, many people found it hard to condemn them.

Furthermore, the golden age of mass communications had dawned. Radio and newsreels transported stories around America in a flash. One side effect of this was the beginning of the culture of celebrity. John Dillinger was among the first of the celebrity criminals, his exploits followed as keenly as those of any Hollywood film star.

John Herbert Dillinger was born in Indianapolis on 22 June 1903. He grew up in the middle-class Oak Hill neighbourhood. His father, John Wilson Dillinger, was a hard-working grocer. His mother died of a stroke when he was only three years old. His sixteen-year-old sister Audrey took over the running of the family for a while, and later John Sr remarried. Much of John's upbringing, however, was left to his father, who would alternate between being a strict disciplinarian and spoiling his son with expensive toys.

Gang rape

This confusing combination may well have been a factor in John Jr growing up to be a difficult, rebellious child. He formed his own gang of local kids, known as the Dirty Dozen. They stole coal from passing freight trains and got into trouble. A more dangerous side to the young Dillinger's nature emerged when he and another boy tied a friend down in a nearby wood mill and turned on the circular saw. Dillinger stopped the saw only when it was inches from cutting into his friend's body. Aged thirteen, Dillinger and some friends gang-raped a local girl.

Dillinger left school aged sixteen and got a job as a mechanic, leading a wild lifestyle when he was not in work. His father had tried hard to make him toe the line. Now he thought it was time for drastic action: he sold up and moved the

John Dillinger was among the first of the celebrity criminals, his exploits followed as keenly as those of any Hollywood film star.

whole family to a farm near Mooresville, Indiana. However, John reacted no better to rural life than he had to the city and soon got into trouble again.

Dillinger was arrested for stealing a car and decided to avoid prosecution by joining the navy. This only lasted a matter of months, however, before he deserted his ship when it docked in Boston. Returning to Mooresville, he married sixteen-year-old Beryl Hovius in 1924. He then became friends with a man named Ed Singleton, the town pool shark. Together they tried to rob a Mooresville grocer, but were caught in the act. Singleton pleaded not guilty, stood trial and was sentenced to two years. [illegible] father's advice confessed

Dillinger's court case was followed by millions of Americans as it was reported on the new and immensely popular technology of the radio

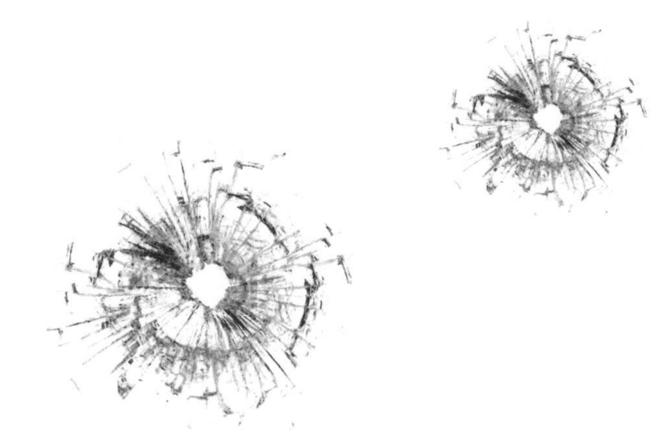

and ended up being sentenced to ten to twenty years in the Indiana State Prison. The harshness of the sentence seems to have turned Dillinger against society once and for all.

Escape and capture

While inside, Dillinger made repeated attempts to escape. He also met up with several more experienced criminals who would have a big influence on his subsequent career. Chief among them were two bank robbers, Harry Pierpoint and Homer Van Meter. Much of their time was spent discussing means of escape. They found a corrupt guard: all they needed was for someone on the outside to bribe the guard to bring some guns into the prison.

The chance came when Dillinger was suddenly paroled ahead of time on 10 May 1933, the reason being that his stepmother was desperately ill. On the outside, Dillinger laid plans to spring his friends from jail. Then, a few days before the planned jailbreak, he robbed a bank in Bluffton, Ohio. He was arrested and sent back to jail in Lima, Ohio, to await trial.

While he was in jail the police searched him and found a document that seemed to be a plan for a prison break. Dillinger denied it and, before the police could get to the bottom of it, eight of Dillinger's friends escaped from the Indiana State Prison, using the guns that had been smuggled into their cells. During their escape, they shot two guards. On 12 October, three of the escaped prisoners repaid the favour and busted Dillinger out of prison, shooting a sheriff in the process.

Now the Dillinger gang swung into action with a vengeance. They pulled several bank robberies. They raided the police arsenals at Auburn, Indiana, and Peru, Indiana, stealing several machine guns, rifles, ammunition and bulletproof vests. Their robberies became ever more high profile. Then, during a raid on a Chicago bank that December, a police officer was killed. Every cop in the country was on the lookout for the gang, but they now had plenty of money and headed to Florida for Christmas and New Year.

Weapons arsenal

Next, they decided to head west to Tucson, Arizona. On the way, however, Dillinger could not resist robbing a bank in Gary, Indiana. This time Dillinger himself shot and killed a policeman as he made his getaway. When they arrived in Tucson, the gang found that they were not as anonymous as they had hoped. A local fireman identified them and soon they were arrested. They were found in possession of three Thompson submachine guns, two Winchester rifles mounted as machine guns, five bulletproof vests and the vast sum of more than twenty-five thousand dollars in cash, part of it from the Chicago robbery.

Dillinger was taken back east to the county jail in Crown Point, Indiana, to await trial for the murder of the police officer. The jail was said to be 'escape proof'. However, on 3 March 1934, Dillinger demonstrated that, as long as it has human beings running it, no jail is truly escape proof. He made a replica gun out of wood, then coloured it black with boot polish. He used the replica gun to force a prison officer to give him a real gun. With the help of another inmate, he took several hostages and drove out of the prison in the governor's own car.

This sensational sting made Dillinger an even bigger hero in the public eye. It also made J. Edgar Hoover's newly formed FBI ever more determined to catch him. A nationwide manhunt began. Pierpoint had been arrested in Tucson and subsequently executed. However, Van Meter was still on the loose and Dillinger teamed up with him. He formed a new gang featuring the murderous talents of Lester Gillis a.k.a. Baby Face Nelson, a man never happier than with a machine gun in his hand. They continued where the old gang had left off, robbing a series of banks, and engaging in another shoot-out with the FBI, this time in St Paul, Minnesota.

John Dillinger, under heavy escort, en route to Indiana by air to answer charges of murdering a policeman in a hold-up

The game is up

Following the shoot-out, in which Dillinger was wounded, the gang went on the run again. They robbed a police station of guns and bulletproof vests before heading to a resort lodge called Little Bohemia, near Rhinelander, Wisconsin, where they planned to hide out for a while. However, the FBI received a tip-off and arrived en masse at Little Bohemia. Once again, it looked as if the game was up for Dillinger. However, the attempted arrest went disastrously wrong. The FBI killed an innocent bystander, Baby Face Nelson killed an FBI agent and all the gangsters got away.

Dillinger's fame was now at its zenith. Perhaps beginning to believe his own publicity, he returned to Chicago, had some minor plastic surgery and began to thumb his nose at the law,

A relaxed Dillinger in prison, surrounded by people eager to get a photograph with him. His celebrity was never in doubt

regularly appearing in public to watch the Chicago Cubs play baseball, or to visit nightclubs. Finally, however, he fell victim not to FBI ingenuity but to the greed of his fellow criminal. A brothel-keeper named Anna Sage, a friend of Dillinger's new girlfriend Polly Hamilton, sold him out.

On the night of Sunday 22 July, FBI agents were waiting as Dillinger, with Sage and Hamilton on either side, walked out of a theatre. Dillinger quickly realized what was happening and grabbed a pistol from his right trouser pocket as he ran towards the alley. Five shots were fired from the guns of three FBI agents. Three of the shots hit Dillinger and he fell face down on the pavement, dead at last.

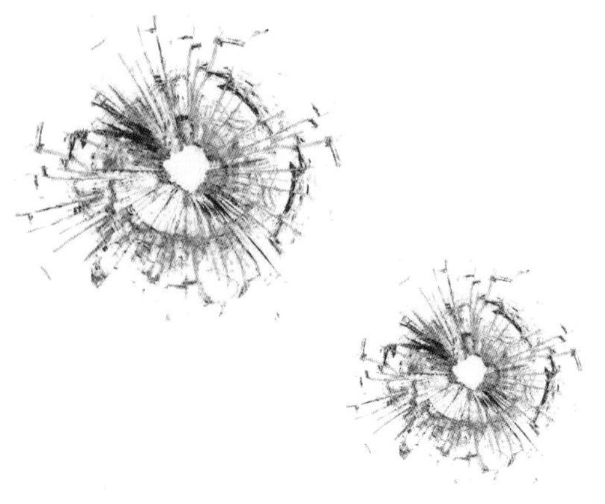

Charles 'Pretty Boy' Floyd

Oklahoma's 'Pretty Boy' Floyd provides the link between the semi-legendary outlaws of the Old West – Jesse James, Wild Bill Hickok to name but a few – and the gangsters of the early twentieth century; Al Capone and Dutch Schulz, for example. Essentially, Pretty Boy Floyd was an outlaw who simply found cars more efficient than horses when it came to running from the law.

Charles Arthur Floyd was born in Bartow County, Georgia, on 3 February 1904, the fourth of eight children born to Walter Lee and Minnie Floyd, hard-working rural Baptists. In 1911, when Charles was seven, Walter Lee decided to move the family to Oklahoma, where he heard there was work in the cotton fields. The family settled in the Cookson Hills and became tenant farmers. Through immense hard work they prospered. Walter eventually opened a general store in the town of Akins. At first Charles seemed to be one more hard-working member of the family, leaving school after the sixth grade to help out with the business.

A changed man

All this changed in 1919, when Charles set off to the harvest fields of Kansas and Oklahoma to make some money. Working in the fields, he fell in with a rough crowd of drifters and vagabonds. When he returned he was a changed man. He started getting into fights and hanging around the local pool hall. He then met his wife, Ruby, and appeared to go straight for a while, but it was not to last. The two set up home and had a baby, Charles Dempsey Floyd and Charles Sr went back to working in the fields, but with an increasing sense of dissatisfaction. He met a petty criminal called John Hilderbrand, who told him how he had robbed a manufacturing company in St Louis of $1,900. Hilderbrand encouraged Charles to join him in carrying out future raids. In August 1925, Charles decided to give it a try. He left home and carried out several successful robberies.

Unfortunately, the duo then made the classic mistake of inexperienced crooks. They bought an expensive car, a new Studebaker, and cruised around the streets of Fort Smith, Arkansas. This soon attracted the suspicion of the police and, before long, Charles was arrested, found guilty for a variety of robberies and sentenced to three years in prison. At his trial the clerk to the court described Charles as 'a mere boy – a pretty boy with apple cheeks' – and a nickname was born, no matter that Charles himself absolutely hated it.

Restroom escape

In prison Charles met many, more experienced, criminals, who urged him to come in with them when he was released. At first Charles wavered, but when he learned that his wife had divorced him, his mind was made up. On release he headed straight for Kansas City, then a Mecca for criminals of all sorts. He stayed in a boarding house popular with criminals, and there met Beulah 'Juanita' Baird, who became his girlfriend. Before long he had hooked up with the Jim Bradley Gang and joined them in a series of raids on banks across Ohio.

At first they were successful, but on 8 March 1930, their luck ran out and they were arrested

Pretty Boy Floyd's apple cheeks belied a criminal mind, but his destruction of banks' paperwork did mean he had more of a claim to the Robin Hood legend than most

by the cops in Akron, Ohio, following a gun battle. This time Floyd was sentenced to fifteen years in prison. However, en route to the penitentiary at Columbus, he performed one of the stunts that was to make his name. During a pit-stop on the journey, Floyd talked his guards into uncuffing him so that he could use the restroom. He smashed the window, jumped out and escaped, making it all the way back to Kansas City.

There he found a new partner, William Miller (a.k.a. Billy the Baby Face Killer). The two of them, along with Juanita, set off to rob banks across the east and south. Once again, though, Floyd met his comeuppance in Ohio. The law caught up with them and there was a shoot-out. Miller was killed and Juanita injured, but Floyd himself managed to escape.

Folk hero

He returned to the Cookson Hills where folk had little love for the law and would protect him. Over the next year or so, Floyd carried out an enormous number of bank robberies – over fifty in 1931 alone. These were the exploits that made him a folk hero, because when he robbed banks, he would also make a point of destroying any mortgage documents he could find. This made him very popular with local farmers as, during these Depression years, the banks were busily foreclosing on mortgages.

During this time, Floyd also reunited himself

When he robbed banks, he would also make a point of destroying any mortgage documents he could find. This made him very popular with local farmers as, during these Depression years, the banks were busily foreclosing on mortgages.

with his wife and son. She had remarried but fell in love with Floyd once more, and left her husband to live as a family with Floyd in Fort Smith, Arkansas, where they adopted the alias of Mr and Mrs Charles Douglas.

This was an unusually happy and contented period in Floyd's life. However, after six months, Ruby suggested that they move to Tulsa, Oklahoma, and there they were turned over to the police by informants eager for the reward money placed on Floyd's head. Once again, though, Floyd managed to escape the law by the narrowest of margins. He returned to the hills and soon became confident enough to give an interview to a reporter, one that helped to ensure that he became a legend.

FBI pursuit

In 1933, Floyd decided to get back into big time crime and headed for Kansas City with his new partner, Adam Richetti. While he was there, on 17 June 1933, an incident known as the Kansas City Massacre took place. This was a gun battle between mobsters and the FBI, in which several FBI agents were shot dead. It is very doubtful that Floyd was actually there, but FBI chief J. Edgar Hoover claimed that he had been, and from this point on Floyd was a major target for the FBI.

He fled to Buffalo, New York. In October 1934, following the death of John Dillinger, Floyd was officially named Public Enemy Number One. The FBI agent who shot Dillinger, Melvin Purvis, was set on his trail.

Floyd decided to flee to Mexico. On the way there, passing through Ohio on 18 October, his car crashed into a ditch. The police stumbled on the car and Floyd fled on foot into a nearby forest. Purvis was notified immediately and FBI agents combed the area. After four days on the run, Purvis finally tracked Floyd down and shot him dead as he tried to escape. After his death, Floyd's body was shipped to Cookson Hills where more than twenty thousand people attended his funeral.

George 'Machine Gun' Kelly

George 'Machine Gun' Kelly was one of several celebrity gangsters active during the era of Prohibition. An undistinguished man in early life, when he turned to crime he became famous, largely as a result of his wife Kathryn's relentless publicity campaign on his behalf. Kelly committed a series of flamboyant bank robberies before kidnapping a millionaire, which led to a national manhunt and his eventual capture. He died in 1954, while serving out a sentence of life imprisonment.

Kelly was born George Kelly Barnes on 18 July 1895 in Memphis, Tennessee. Unlike most gangsters of the period, he was not tempted into a life of crime through growing up in poverty; on the contrary, his father was an insurance company executive and he came from a wealthy, middle-class family. As a child, Kelly was very fond of his mother, but did not get on with his father. During his teenage years, he found out that his father was having an affair and, when his mother died while he was in high school, he blamed his father for her death.

The bootlegging trade

After leaving high school, Kelly enrolled at Mississippi State University to study agriculture. He was not a good student, and showed no interest in his work. When he met a girl called Geneva Ramsey and fell in love, he decided to quit university and marry her. The couple went on to have two children, and Kelly had to support his new family. He worked as a cab driver in Memphis for a while, but his earnings were not enough, and he soon began to look around for other opportunities. Before long, he met a local gangster and turned to crime, working in the bootlegging trade and changing his name so as not to bring shame on his respectable family.

Kelly was arrested several times as a result of his illegal activities, and each time his wife and other relatives had to bail him out. He began drinking heavily. To get him away from his underground cronies, the family moved to Kansas City, where for a short time Kelly went straight and worked in a grocery store, before his

Kelly went on to perform a series of bank robberies, resulting in a flurry of 'Wanted' posters that emphasized his prowess as an 'expert machine gunner'.

Behind every great man... Kathryn Thorne was Kelly's unofficial public relations manager, building him a fearsome reputation as a highly skilled machine gunner

wife found out that he was stealing from the till. Realizing that he was incapable of staying in a straight job, his wife left him, and the couple later divorced.

Now on his own, Kelly stayed in Kansas City and began to build up a bootlegging business there. He gained a reputation in the trade, expanding his operations across several states, but in 1927 he was caught and arrested. The following year, he was sentenced to three years imprisonment for smuggling liquor into an Indian reservation. He then served out another sentence for bootlegging before moving to Oklahoma City, where he met his future partner in crime.

The outlaw bride – and PR girl

Kathryn Thorne was the mistress of a bootlegger named Steve Anderson, but she was also a hardened criminal in her own right. She came from a family of outlaws: her mother was a bootlegger, her aunt a prostitute and several other members were known to police for robbery offences. Thorne was a divorcee who had been married twice, and it was rumoured that she had shot her second husband dead for infidelity. Kelly immediately became enamoured of the worldly wise Thorne, and the pair were married in 1930. From that time on, Kelly rose from being a small-time criminal to a well-known gangster, reaching a pinnacle of infamy when he became 'Public Enemy Number One'.

Thorne bought her husband his first machine gun and encouraged him to practise shooting it, distributing the used cartridges to the denizens of underground drinking clubs as souvenirs from 'Machine Gun' Kelly. In this way, she built up a reputation for her husband as a cold-blooded killer and an expert gunman. Kelly went on to perform a series of bank robberies, resulting in a series of 'Wanted' posters that emphasized his prowess as an 'expert machine gunner'. The public was terrified, and Kelly hit the headlines as America's most wanted gangster.

In July 1933, Kelly kidnapped a wealthy oil man, Charles Urschel. He demanded a ransom of

two hundred thousand dollars. Once the money was delivered, Urschel was freed. A huge investigation was launched, aided by Urschel, who had carefully laid as many clues as he could during his ordeal. Kelly and his cronies were now on the run.

The law closes in

The other members of the Kelly gang were soon arrested and charged as accomplices in the kidnap. Meanwhile, Kelly and his wife moved around from state to state, living a life of luxury on the ransom money. However, the police were steadily closing in. When the couple paid a visit to an old friend in Memphis, the FBI managed to catch up with them, surrounding the house and forcing their way in. Kelly, terrified of being killed, was reported to have pleaded for mercy. The couple was arrested, tried and convicted. They both received life sentences.

Initially, Kelly was jailed at Leavenworth in Kansas, but while he was there he continually boasted about how he would escape from the prison. His threats were taken seriously, and in 1934 he was transferred to Alcatraz. There, he continued to boast, this time about crimes he had never committed, which irritated his fellow prisoners immensely but in most ways he served out his sentence as a model prisoner. In 1951, he was sent back to Leavenworth. Three years later, on 18 July – which happened to be his birthday – he died of a heart attack.

Kelly's trial was high profile – and well guarded

Ned Kelly

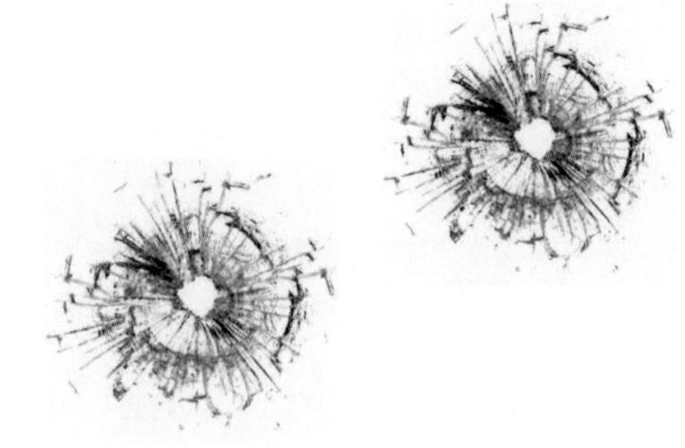

Ned Kelly is perhaps the most famous folk hero of Australia. He was a bushranger who rose from poverty during the late nineteenth century to become a thorn in the side of the police. His career of crime, and his letters to the press explaining his actions, drew attention to the authorities' persecution of the country's poorest farming families, who were trying to scratch a living in the harsh conditions of the Australian outback at the time.

Kelly was born near Melbourne in Beveridge, Victoria, in 1854. His parents, John and Ellen, were Irish immigrants; his father was an ex-convict, now doing his best to go straight. Ned was the eldest boy, and the third of eight children. As a child, he saved a schoolmate from drowning, and for his bravery was awarded a green sash, which he later wore under his armour when he clashed with police.

As the twelve-year-old head of the family, Ned was faced with an impossible task. He did his best, struggling to earn a living in the harsh conditions of the country

The outlaw clan

When Ned was twelve years old, his father died, and the family moved to Glenrowan in Victoria, which today is known as 'Kelly Country'. Ned was forced to leave school to provide for his large family. The family became 'selectors', landless farmers who were allowed to live on small, often barren areas of land set aside by the government. The idea was that the selectors could improve the property and buy the land bit by bit, but inevitably, they were too poor to make the necessary improvements, and often the land was taken back from them. Faced with ruin, the selectors sometimes took to stealing livestock from richer farmers, and then escaping into the bush and living as 'bushrangers' – bandits and cattle rustlers.

Ned Kelly was Australia's best-known outlaw. This picture was taken the day before he was hanged at the Old Melbourne jail, in November 1880, aged just twenty-five years

As the twelve-year-old head of the family, Ned was faced with an impossible task. He did his best, struggling to earn a living in the harsh weather conditions of the country. As well as the poverty, the Kelly family had to endure persecution by the police, because their mother, Ellen Quinn, came from an extended family of outlaws that had a reputation in the area. The Kellys were constantly being charged with one offence or another, although often when the cases came to court the charges did not stick.

The battle of Stringy Bark Creek

At the age of fourteen, Ned was arrested for assaulting a pig farmer, but found not guilty. The following year, he was again arrested for assault, and this time he was sentenced to six months' hard labour. After he was released, he was arrested again for being in possession of a stolen horse, although it seems that he did not know the horse was stolen. This time, he was sentenced to three years in prison.

Ned Kelly's infamous armour was made from beaten-out farm implements

In 1878, a policeman, Constable Alexander Fitzpatrick, assaulted Kelly's sister, Ellen, at the family's home. Fitzpatrick then accused Kelly of trying to murder him. Kelly fled with his brother Dan into the bush. Some months later, they and their friends Joe Byrne and Steve Hart, came across police camped at a place called Stringy Bark Creek. A fight ensued and, in the process of it, Kelly shot dead three policemen. From that time on, Kelly was a fully fledged outlaw, constantly on the run. Police put up a huge reward for his capture, but the Kelly Gang, as they became known, had many friends in the area, and nobody turned them in.

Home-made armour

In 1879, having run short of funds, Kelly robbed a bank at Euroa. The same year, he also committed a bank robbery at Jerilderie. He then composed a long letter to the press, which became known as the 'Jerilderie Letter'. It set out his views on the police and the way they had treated his family, and listing the way in which Protestant police ill-treated Catholic families in Australia. It also predicted uprisings in Australia, Ireland and the US against the persecution that he felt the Catholics had suffered.

In 1880, Kelly and his men came back to Glenrowan, bringing armour that they had fashioned themselves. The armour had been made out of agricultural machinery parts, and weighed about eighty pounds per suit. The gang held about sixty hostages prisoner in a local inn, and then attempted to derail a police train. The plan was foiled by a hostage, schoolmaster

A mock-up of the Kelly Gang's last stand still draws crowds of tourists each year, proving the enduring appeal of this gang of desperadoes

Thomas Curnow, who stood on the rails waving a red scarf and holding a lighted candle to warn away the train.

An almighty shoot-out

When police caught up with the Kelly Gang at Glenrowan, there was an almighty shoot-out, in which Kelly himself was shot many times in the legs, the only part of him not protected by his armour. Other gang members, namely Dan Kelly, Joe Byrne and Steve Hart, died in the inn. Ned managed to survive his injuries long enough to stand trial, and was later sentenced to death. A petition was signed by over thirty thousand people, asking for his sentence to be repealed, but it was to no avail. The flamboyant Ned Kelly was hanged on 11 November 1880, at the age of twenty-five.

After his death, Kelly became a folk hero in his native land. During his life, Kelly had developed a reputation as a polite man who treated his neighbours well. The hounding of his family by the police had also attracted a great deal of sympathy from the public. The outcry that accompanied his hanging eventually caused the authorities to launch an enquiry, and as a result all the police officers connected with the case were either dismissed or brought down in rank.

Freedom fighter... or common criminal?

Today, Kelly is a controversial figure. Some see him as a common criminal who robbed and murdered for his own gain; but to others, he is a romantic figure who continues to embody the Australian settlers' values of self-reliance, independence and freedom from persecution in a land of opportunity.

COVERT SPIES

During the Cold War, the shadowy world of espionage was full of highly intelligent spies: people who knew how to double-cross, lie, cheat and cover their tracks so that they could continue their secret activities for years. Many of them, such as the physicist Klaus Fuchs, were experts in their field, with specialist knowledge that made them indispensable to the spy networks for which they worked. Others, such as the British Cambridge spies – Philby, Burgess, Maclean and Blunt – were highly educated individuals from the upper echelons of society.

What characterized them all, and other more recent spies such as Christopher Boyce, was a hostile, cynical attitude towards the governments that they served. In most cases, their initial rationale seems to have been in part political, or at least the result of a kind of generalized rage at the hypocrisies of the social class they belonged to. (Interestingly, two American spies – Aldrich Ames in the Cold War period, and Christopher Boyce in the 1970s – were sons of CIA agents. They both dropped out of college and were rescued by their fathers, who got them jobs in the service.) At the same time, many of them seem to have been motivated by a need for excitement and adventure; just as with the other criminal masterminds in this book, their intelligence went hand in hand with a rebellious streak. However, in nearly every instance, their values seemed to become blurred over a period of time, so that it was no longer clear why they were acting as they did: whether out of self-interest, a belief in the greater good or – as Christopher Boyce put it – a simple 'lust for adventure'.

Aldrich Ames

Aldrich Ames, a CIA official, was one of the most damaging spies ever to work at the agency. In order to fund his lavish lifestyle, he sold secrets to the Soviet Union, which resulted in the arrest and execution of many of his colleagues by the KGB. After thirty-one years with the CIA, during which time he spent almost ten years spying for the Russians, he was eventually caught. In 1994, he received a life sentence, while his Colombian-born second wife, Maria del Rosario, was sentenced to five years in prison.

Ames was born in 1941 in Wisconsin. His mother, Rachel, was a high-school teacher. While he was growing up, his father, Carleton Ames, secretly worked for the CIA. The family lived in Burma in the early 1950s, and then returned to the US to live in Washington DC. Aldrich, known as Rick, attended Langley High School, and was keen on drama. During his teenage years, he got a summer job working for the CIA, making fake money for use in training exercises.

Recruiting spies

Rick went on to attend Chicago University, but did not finish his degree because of his drama activities. His father came to the rescue, getting him a job with the CIA in 1962. He began working for a secret branch of the CIA that trained employees to recruit spies. Ames was then sent to Ankara in Turkey to find spies for the agency, posing as an army officer. His acting skills came

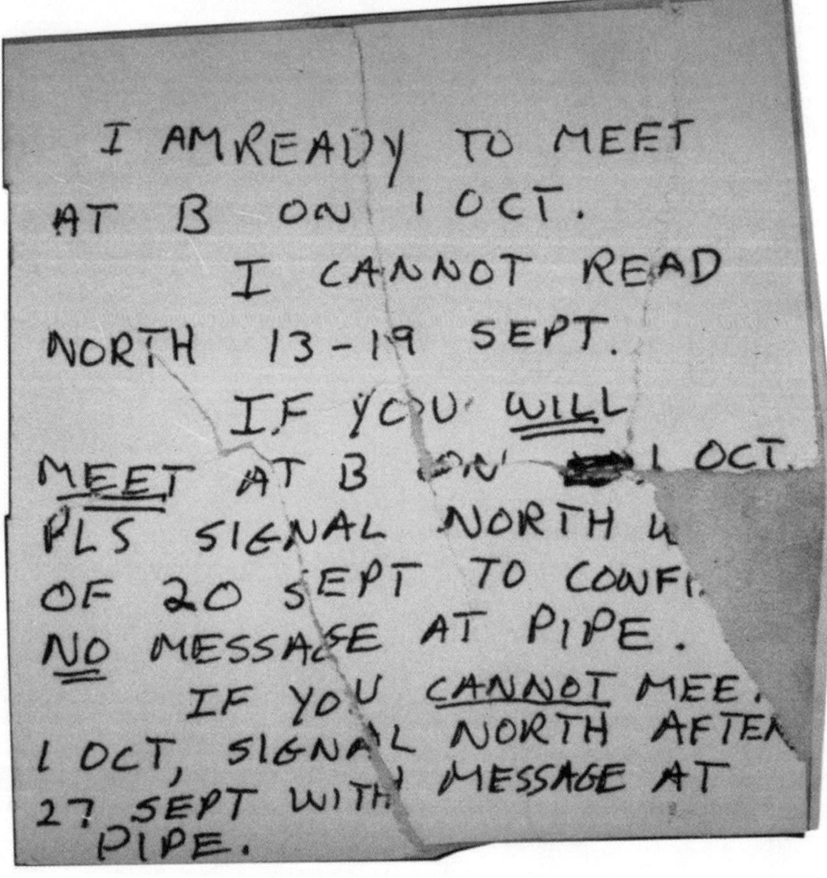
I AM READY TO MEET
AT B ON 1 OCT.
I CANNOT READ
NORTH 13-19 SEPT.
IF YOU WILL
MEET AT B ON 1 OCT.
PLS SIGNAL NORTH
OF 20 SEPT TO CONFI
NO MESSAGE AT PIPE.
IF YOU CANNOT MEE
1 OCT, SIGNAL NORTH AFTE
27 SEPT WITH MESSAGE AT
PIPE.

Note found by the FBI in 1993, in Aldrich Ames' rubbish bin, concerning a meeting with his KGB contact in Bogota, Colombia

The most shocking aspect of this betrayal was that the information he gave the Soviets led to the execution of at least ten of his CIA colleagues in the Soviet Union.

in handy for the job, but he failed to recruit any spies.

Next, the CIA sent him to study Russian, at which he proved more successful. He went on to work in Moscow, New York and Mexico City for the CIA. He began to deal with top-level Russian spies who had defected, and became a high-ranking CIA official. However, by this time he had begun to drink heavily, and had quarrelled with his wife, Nan, who had remained in the US when he was posted to Mexico. Moreover, he was having strong doubts about the policies the CIA were adopting at that period. Contrary to the government's propaganda, he believed that the threat to the United States from the Soviet Union was non-existent, and that the CIA's involvement in Nicaragua, trying to crush the Sandinista rebels, was entirely wrong.

Love and betrayal

In Mexico City, he met Maria del Rosario Casas Dupuy, who worked as the cultural attaché for the Colombian embassy there. Ames and Rosario began to go out together and soon fell in love. However, in 1983 he was called back to New York with a promotion, as head of counter-intelligence in Soviet operations.

Once in the job, Ames began to realize the extent of the US's spy system in the Soviet Union. He had information on every aspect of it, including the numerous Russian operatives who secretly worked for the CIA. With his faith in the agency gone, and with mounting personal pressures – Rosario had followed him to New York and he was negotiating a divorce with his first wife – he began to think about ways in which he could make extra money. His new girlfriend was a spendthrift, and he was having trouble keeping up with her extravagant ways; additionally, his wife had kept many of their joint assets, and he owed her money as part of the divorce settlement.

Ames now began to sell the names of Russians spying for the CIA. Over a period of several years he received as much as two and a half million dollars from the KGB, in return for information on over a hundred US intelligence operations. The most shocking aspect of this betrayal was that the information he gave the Soviets led to the execution of at least ten of his CIA colleagues in the Soviet Union.

Shot in the head

Of the twenty-five 'sources' that Ames named, ten were sentenced to what the Russians called 'vyshaya mera' ('the highest measure of punishment'). They were taken to a cell, made to kneel and then shot in the back of the head so that their faces were completely destroyed. Afterwards, they were buried in unmarked graves, so that their relatives could not mourn them properly.

Most of the Russian operatives were not personally known to Ames, but there was one close friend whom he betrayed – not once, but twice. This was Sergey Fedorenko, who had known Ames since his days in New York. Fedorenko knew that the KGB suspected him of spying (the result of Ames' tip-off), so he contacted his friend and asked for help in moving to the US. At a secret meeting between the two, Ames promised he would do his best, but immediately afterwards telephoned his superiors and told them what had happened.

Meanwhile, the CIA was beginning to realize that something was wrong in the organization. As more and more operations failed, it soon became clear that someone in the know was selling their secrets to the Russians. However, it took a long time for the searchlight to fall on Ames, even though it was clear that his lifestyle was way above what his salary could pay for. Instead of looking at their personnel, the CIA concentrated on technical problems, such as code breaking, to explain what had gone wrong. It was not until the FBI were called in that Ames became a prime suspect. The FBI put him under constant surveillance, and just before he and Rosario, now his wife, were due to fly to Moscow, they arrested the pair and charged them with providing classified information to the KGB.

Both pleaded guilty and, at their trial, Ames was sentenced to life incarceration without parole, while Rosario received a sentence of sixty-three months. Today, Ames continues to serve out his sentence. After serving hers, Rosario returned to live in Colombia.

Not caring who he hurt – American or Russian – Ames found spying the most lucrative way to fund his lifestyle

Christopher Boyce and Andrew Daulton Lee

Christopher Boyce was a CIA employee who had access to highly classified information from the Pine Gap spy satellite, which was based in Australia. He was caught selling secrets to the Russians, and received a forty-year prison sentence. His defence was from an apparently moral standpoint – that the US government was not sharing secret information with the Australian government, which they had signed an agreement to do. He also believed that the CIA wanted to destabilize the socialist government of Australian prime minister Gough Whitlam.

However, during his trial it emerged that Boyce's real reasons for spying were somewhat unclear. Although he despised the US government, he was not politically involved with any particular group; nor did he make a great deal of money from his spying activities. It seems possible that, ultimately, his career as a spy was motivated by nothing more than a lust for adventure.

The young daredevil

Christopher Boyce was born in 1953 in Santa Monica, California. His father Charles had at one time been an FBI agent, but was now working in the aircraft industry. His mother Noreen was a devout Catholic who did not believe in contraception, and consequently the couple went on to have eight more children. Christopher was brought up in a strongly moral, religious atmosphere and was taught to be a patriotic, all-American boy.

The young Christopher did well in school, and became an altar boy at church. He loved the outdoor life, and was well known to everyone for his daredevil exploits. He became a good-looking teenager, and was generally popular.

Christopher met his friend Andrew Daulton Lee at church, where the pair served as altar boys. They spent a lot of time together, and attended the same high school. They took up falconry, developing a passion for training birds. Lee was also enjoying woodwork at school, and becoming an excellent carpenter. However, despite his talent, Lee felt inferior: he was short, he had acne and he thought himself unattractive to girls.

Government secrets

As teenagers, Boyce and Lee both began to lose interest in school work. Boyce started to lose his Catholic faith and to question his patriotism. Lee

Christopher Boyce – denied the freedom he so loved as exemplified by his passion for falconry

Although Boyce despised the US government, he was not politically involved with any particular group; nor did he make a great deal of money from his spying activities. It seems possible that, ultimately, his career as a spy was motivated by nothing more than a lust for adventure.

took to selling drugs, supplying marijuana and cocaine to girls in exchange for sex. When the boys left high school, Lee stepped up his drug dealing, especially the cocaine, and became known as 'The Snowman'. Boyce enrolled in college, but kept dropping out.

At this point, Charles Boyce intervened on behalf of his son, getting a friend to hire Chris at an aerospace company called TWR. This was a private company that was involved in operating US spy satellites. Boyce became a general clerk in the company, dealing with classified information. An intelligent young man who actually read the material carefully, he was disgusted to find that the US government was withholding information gathered from spy satellites; in particular, they had signed an agreement with the Australian government, and were not passing on vital data. According to Boyce, this was because the Australian government was headed by a socialist, Gough Whitlam. Boyce was even more enraged when he found out that the CIA was infiltrating the Australian labour unions. However, rather than showing his disapproval through protest, Boyce decided on another course of action. He would sell the secrets to the Russians. That way, he would not only salve his political conscience, but he would also make some money.

Lust for adventure

Boyce discussed his plans with Lee, who by that time was getting into a great deal of trouble because of his drug dealing activities. Lee had been in prison, and was frightened of returning. He needed another line of business fast. The pair hatched a plot together whereby Lee would travel to the Soviet embassy in Mexico City and tell them about Boyce's access to classified information. This Lee did, showing evidence of his friend's employment.

The Soviets immediately showed interest, and within a short time Lee was dropping off information, and receiving packets of money, for his friend Boyce, who now became known as 'The Falcon'. Lee met a Soviet official in public, using passwords and designated drop-off points. Boyce and Lee started to make money, but before long they were squabbling over it. Lee had by now become a heroin addict, and Boyce suspected that he was not getting his fair share of the cash. Boyce was getting tired of the whole business of selling secrets, and was planning to leave TWR and go to college. In the meantime, he gave Lee some photographs of a new satellite, the Pyramider, that the US was planning to build.

Down Mexico way

When Lee took the photos down to Mexico City, trouble ensued. Lee was arrested by Mexican police and charged with murdering a policeman. After a harrowing experience in a Mexican jail, Lee was handed over to the FBI, where his story – that he was working for the CIA – began to seriously unravel.

Not long afterwards, Chris Boyce was arrested. He was brought to trial, and told the jury the truth about his spying activities. He added that he had never told Lee that they were working for the CIA. He was given a forty-year sentence. Lee was tried separately, and was given life imprisonment.

In 1980, Boyce escaped and went on the run, living free for over a year and working at a tree nursery before committing a series of bank robberies. He was eventually caught and sent back to prison. Lee was paroled in 1998, and Boyce in 2003.

Sean Penn (left) and Timothy Hutton in the film The Falcon and the Snowman *– the story of Boyce and Lee*

The Cambridge Spies

During the years of the Cold War, the fraught, ideological battle between the western democracies and the communist states was conducted in secret by an army of spies trading in information. Not only that, at the end of the war many agents were revealed to have been working for both sides. Their motives varied: some were engaged in this dangerous game for money; others had strong political convictions; and yet others – in a milieu where the means always justified the ends – had lost sight of their moral code altogether. Among the most prominent of these double agents were four young Englishmen recruited from the social elite at Cambridge University. Their names were Kim Philby, Guy Burgess, Donald Maclean and Anthony Blunt.

The 'old boy' network

The four met as students during the 1930s, at a time when the Depression was causing mass unemployment in the west. In this context, the rise of fascism in Germany and Italy was extremely menacing: Hitler and Mussolini were rapidly mobilizing support among a working-class population suffering poverty and social fragmentation in the aftermath of the First World War. In British academic circles, it was widely believed that the western democracies would not provide strong anti-fascist leadership against these demagogues; in fact, it was well known that among the anti-semitic British upper classes there was a good deal of sympathy with the Nazis. Thus, a rising generation of intellectuals looked to the Soviet Union as a bulwark against fascism.

At the same time, the Soviet Union's intelligence agency, the KGB, conceived the plan of recruiting at Britain's most respected universities. They knew that the British establishment operated on an 'old boy' network, in which the children of the upper classes went to fee-paying 'public' schools, then to one or other of the two top universities in the country, Oxford and Cambridge, and from there into high-level jobs in politics, the civil service, the law and so on. In this way, the KGB planned to recruit agents who would be working at the heart of government. Their plan paid off: with the Cambridge spies, they managed to recruit young men who would become important establishment figures with access to extremely sensitive information. Moreover, the 'old boy' network ensured that, for many years, their activities as double agents were never discovered: so snobbish and cliquey was the British establishment that it simply could not bring itself to suspect its own members.

Debonair, charming – yet deadly

The most infamous of the four men was Harold Philby, nicknamed 'Kim' after a character in Rudyard Kipling's *Jungle Book*. He was highly intelligent, and could be debonair and charming, yet few claim to have really known him well. On graduating from Cambridge, he became a newspaper reporter and then went on to work for the British Secret Intelligence Service, where he eventually became head of the anti-Soviet section. All the time, he was reporting back to the KGB, which sometimes resulted in the execution of British spies in the Soviet Union,

and certainly contributed to damaging the Allies' military efforts during the Second World War.

Blunt was another enigmatic figure. Unlike Philby, who was known as a womaniser, Blunt was a homosexual. It is thought that he was recruited by the KGB on a trip to Russia in 1933, and recruited the other agents on his return. An art historian, Blunt became director of the Courtault Institute and art adviser to the Queen, both extremely respected positions. In 1956, he was knighted.

Guy Burgess was another homosexual, who at one time had a sexual relationship with Blunt. A flamboyant character, he was intelligent and charming, but had a serious flaw that made him deeply unreliable: he was an alcoholic. Burgess became a BBC broadcaster and a senior civil servant at the Foreign Office, which gave him access to extremely important people and crucial information.

The fourth spy, Donald Maclean, was a high-level diplomat at the British Embassy in Washington DC, and during the war became one of Stalin's chief informants. His work as a spy helped the Soviets build the atom bomb and assess their capability in the nuclear arms race. He was a tense, nervous man – also an alcoholic – who was a worry to his colleagues Blunt and Philby because they thought that given his unstable mental state, he would crack if interrogated by the British secret services, and land them all in trouble.

The KGB planned to recruit agents who would be working at the heart of government. Their plan paid off: with the Cambridge spies, they managed to recruit young men who would become important establishment figures with access to extremely sensitive information.

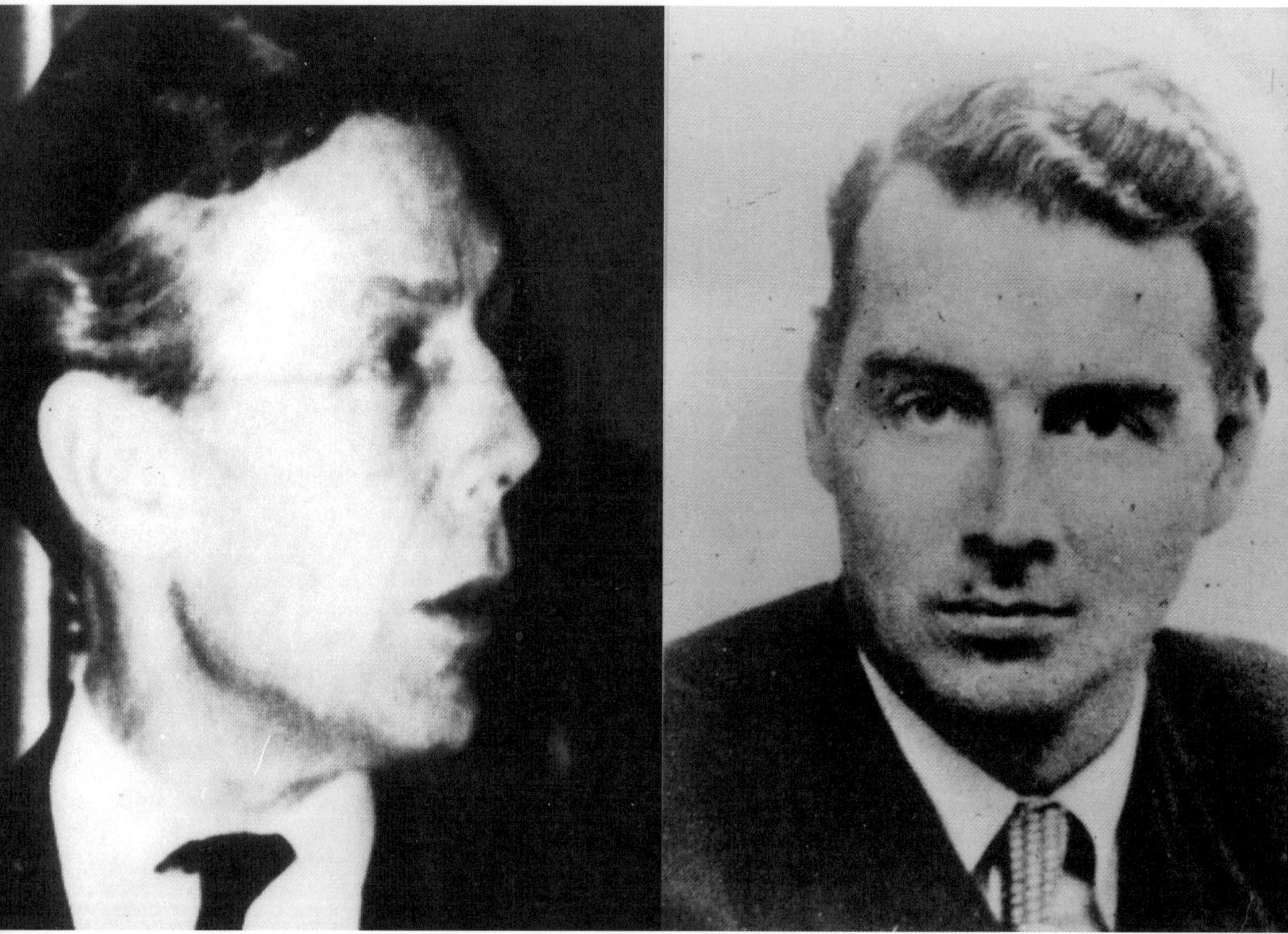

Defecting to the USSR

For many years, the spies' activities were not discovered. Then, in 1949, Robert Lamphere of the FBI found out, through breaking a secret code, that a member of the British embassy was sending messages to the Russians. With pressure mounting, Burgess and Maclean unexpectedly defected to the Soviet Union, leaving Philby to pick up the pieces. Philby remained stoical under questioning from British intelligence, but was forced to resign from his job. He later also defected to the Soviet Union.

Anthony Blunt remained in the country and, in 1964, confessed to his part in the spying operation. However, he was given immunity from prosecution, which was largely to protect the reputation of British intelligence and the British royal family. Many years later, in 1979, Blunt was publicly stripped of his honours, including his knighthood. Even then, he continued to live quietly in England, where he died in 1983.

Moral meltdown

Today, many questions still remain unanswered about the Cambridge spies. It is clear that they did not become traitors to their country for money: none of them appears to have been paid a great deal for his services. At the same time, their political convictions are somewhat unclear; they may have begun their careers as staunch communists, but at the least, one can say that the Cold War was an extremely complex business, and so was their response to it. Recent information from the disbanded Soviet Union has indicated that the Cambridge spies may in fact have been triple agents: that is, British spies working as informers for the Russians, but secretly infiltrating the KGB and reporting back to British intelligence.

Whatever the truth, it seems that ultimately, the deviations and counter-deviations of the Cold War became so tortuous that in the end, a kind of moral meltdown took place. In this context, notions of truth, justice and the greater good appeared to have become simplistic and meaningless – at least to the Cambridge spies, who were at the heart of the ideological battle between western democracy and eastern-bloc communism.

Blunt, Burgess, Philby and Maclean – the idealist Cambridge spies at the height of their spying activities

Klaus Fuchs

Klaus Fuchs was a German-born physicist who was hounded by the Nazis during the 1930s because of his communist beliefs. He left Germany to live in Britain and the US, where he worked on the development of the atom bomb. Ostensibly, he posed as an impartial scientist, but unbeknown to his colleagues, he was passing highly sensitive information to the Soviet Union, at a time when the race was on to develop the atom bomb as the ultimate war weapon. In 1945, the US won the race, detonating the bomb with horrific consequences on Hiroshima.

To this day, no one knows exactly how much Fuchs influenced the outcome of the arms race. Edward Teller, one of the principal figures in developing the hydrogen bomb, believed that Fuchs gave away major secrets, and that he saved the Russians about ten years of their own research as a result. Other commentators, such as the CIA, thought that the time saved was probably much less, perhaps only one or two years. It seems likely, in hindsight, that Fuchs confirmed what the Russians were already working towards, rather than that he gave them entirely new information.

Fleeing the Nazis

Emil Julius Klaus Fuchs was born in Russelsheim, Germany, in 1911, one of four children. The whole family was intensely political but somewhat mentally unstable. His father was a Quaker and took great care in the moral education of his children, but he was not an affectionate man. His mother committed suicide when Fuchs was at college. His sister Elisabeth became a radical activist and met her death by jumping into the path of an oncoming train while being pursued by the Gestapo. His brother Gerhard was also an activist, and was expelled from law school and imprisoned several times. His younger sister Kristel left Germany and studied in the United States, where she was diagnosed as a schizophrenic during her college years. Fuchs later believed himself to be suffering from what he called a 'controlled' form of schizophrenia, and some believe that this condition may have been a factor in his ability to 'compartmentalize' his feelings, such as loyalty to his colleagues, in his work as a spy.

Klaus began his career at Leipzig University, where he studied physics and mathematics. He took a keen interest in politics and joined the Communist Party. In 1933, the Nazis gained power in Germany and began to round up and imprison German communists, forcing Klaus to flee the country. He escaped to Britain and continued his studies there, gaining a doctorate in physics from Bristol University in 1937. He then went on to further study at Edinburgh University.

The Trinity test

At the outbreak of the Second World War, German citizens living in Britain were sent to internment camps, to be held there until the war ended. Fuchs was taken to a camp in Quebec, Canada, but a colleague intervened to persuade the authorities that he was doing important work that would be useful in the war effort, and he was set free. He went to work at the British atomic bomb centre in Birmingham, on a project known as 'tube alloys'. Here, he conducted research with another German physicist who had fled his homeland, Rudolf Peierls.

In 1942, Fuchs became a British citizen. The

Atom spy Dr Klaus Fuchs checks his ticket with an air hostess at London Airport, in June 1959. Fuchs was released from jail in England after serving nine years of his fourteen-year prison sentence for spying

following year, he went to the US to work at Columbia University in New York, on the atom bomb research programme there, the Manhattan Project. From New York, he was sent to another research centre, Los Alamos in New Mexico, where he was involved in developing and testing the atom bomb. He was present at the first atomic bomb test, the Trinity test. At the end of the war, Fuchs returned to Britain and worked in nuclear research at the centre in Harwell.

Soviet spy

It was during his time at 'tube alloys' in Birmingham, England, that Fuchs began to pass information about his work on the project to the Soviet Union. He was contacted by a female

Fuchs later believed himself to be suffering from what he called a 'controlled' form of schizophrenia, and some believe that this condition may have been a factor in his ability to 'compartmentalize' his feelings, such as loyalty to his colleagues, in his work as a spy.

Russian spy, known only as 'the girl from Banbury', and in brief meetings with her, gave her research papers to look at. At this stage, he is thought to have communicated only his own research information. When he moved to New York and started work on the Manhattan Project, he began to give detailed information on the programme in general to Harry Gold, a Soviet spy who worked under the name 'Raymond'. This was not discovered until several years later, when intelligence officers managed to crack Soviet codes in an operation known as the Venona Project. A message was deciphered, reporting on the progress of the atom bomb in the west. It was unclear whether or not Fuchs himself had written the document, but there was

Fuchs was met by his nephew Klaus Kittowski (right) at an airport in East Berlin. Fuchs moved to East Germany immediately after his arrival back from England, and jail

now no doubt that the Russians had infiltrated the Manhattan Project and had known all along what was being developed.

Suspicion soon fell on Klaus Fuchs, and he was investigated by the FBI. At first he denied any involvement, but after a series of interviews he confessed. He was duly brought to trial. In 1950, he was found guilty of passing secrets to the Soviets, and received a prison sentence of fourteen years. After nine years, he was released, and went to work in communist East Germany, at the Institute for Nuclear Physics near Dresden. He married, lived quietly with his wife and worked hard as a scientist. In 1979, he was honoured for his life's work with the Order of Karl Marx. He died in 1988.

TERRORIST MASTERMINDS

In the wake of the horrifying events of 9/11, the issue of terrorism has come to dominate the headlines. The shadowy figures behind these attacks, although they excite disgust, are also fascinating. What are the motives of these men and women who cause so much destruction? Are they essentially political in nature, or is there an emotional pathology that causes them to wreak havoc in the lives of ordinary people? Here, we look at a range of terrorist operators, from powerful leaders like Osama bin Laden to lone oddballs such as 'The Unabomber', Ted Kaczynski.

Although there are many differences between these figures, a surprising number of similarities emerge. In most cases, these are people with a high level of intelligence, coupled with a greater or lesser degree of mental imbalance. There are those from rich, privileged backgrounds, such as Osama bin Laden, the son of a multi-millionaire Saudi Arabian businessman; and Carlos the Jackal, son of a rich Marxist lawyer from Venezuela. These are the rebels who reject the privileges of their background and upbringing, yet constantly reveal the arrogance of their class – and, moreover, have almost limitless funds to bankroll their pet projects. Then there are the loners, men like Ted Kaczynski and Timothy McVeigh, who kill as a kind of revenge for what they sense as their exclusion from the mainstream of social life. What characterizes all of these individuals is their inability to empathize with human suffering, or to tolerate ways of life, beliefs and values other than their own – despite the fact that they are, on the whole, among the most intelligent of criminals.

Osama bin Laden

Before the bombing of the World Trade Center in New York on 11 September 2001, the name Osama bin Laden was not well known to the general public. However, when he emerged as the prime suspect in masterminding this horrific atrocity, everyone suddenly wanted to know the history of a man capable of organizing such a crime. It transpired that bin Laden was the scion of a super-rich Saudi family, who had turned to religious fundamentalism and had for many years been involved in anti-American terrorist activity, even persuading his followers to commit suicide for the cause. Today, bin Laden is known as 'the most wanted man in the world', but has continued to elude capture, broadcasting on Arab television from time to time from secret locations around the globe.

Osama bin Laden was born in 1957, the son of a hugely wealthy Saudi Arabian billionaire named Muhammad Awad bin Laden. His father had begun life as a poor manual worker and risen to become the head of a huge construction business; he was closely connected with the Saudi royal family, for whom he had built a number of luxurious palaces. Osama is thought to be Muhammad's seventeenth son, one of fifty-four siblings. The reason the family was so large was that Muhammad married ten times, and under Islamic law was allowed to have four wives at a time. Osama's mother, Hamida al-Attas, was Muhammad's tenth wife.

Bankrolling the radicals

Osama grew up in the Sunni Muslim faith. He attended college in Beirut, Lebanon, where he reportedly led a sociable student life, going out to bars and clubs. He gained a degree in civil engineering, and also studied business administration. When his father died, he inherited a fortune of about twenty-five million dollars, and married his first wife (who was also his cousin), Najwah Ghanem. He also married four other women, under Islamic law, and divorced one of them. He is thought to have fathered over twenty children, and at least three of his sons are today reported to be active in terrorist organizations.

Bin Laden's vast wealth gave him the opportunity to sponsor various political causes, including that of the Mujahedeen, an organization of Muslims fighting the Soviet Union after the invasion of Afghanistan in 1979. His political group was known as Maktab al-Khadamat (MAK), and provided arms, money and soldiers for the war. It was supported by the Saudi and Pakistani governments. A decade later, bin Laden had left MAK and built up a more militant organization, al-Qaeda, and became openly critical of the Saudi government's links with the US, especially the presence of US military bases in Saudi Arabia. Eventually, the Saudi Arabian government expelled bin Laden, and later stripped him of his citizenship.

Osama bin Laden is the mastermind's mastermind, having wealth, power and political conviction behind his plans

It transpired that bin Laden was the scion of a super-rich Saudi family, who had turned to religious fundamentalism.

Terrorist atrocities

Bin Laden established a new base in Sudan, investing in construction and agricultural companies, and building up training camps in the countryside. Around this time, he masterminded several terrorist attacks on military bases in Saudi Arabia. Under mounting international pressure, the Sudanese government expelled him, and he moved to Afghanistan, where he became closely linked to the fundamentalist Muslim government known as the Taliban. Once again, bin Laden's money endeared him to the government, and he was able to plan several more terrorist attacks, protected by his new friends.

Bin Laden is thought to be behind the 1992 bombing of the Gold Mihor Hotel in Aden, Yemen, that killed three people. A few days before, a large group of US soldiers had been staying there. He is also thought to have been involved in the attempt to bomb the World Trade Center in 1993. The 1997 killing of tourists in Luxor, Egypt, which was perpetrated by an Egyptian Islamic group, is also believed to have been funded by bin Laden. In 2000, the bombing of a US ship, the USS *Cole*, in Aden, Yemen, is also attributed to bin Laden.

In 1998, bin Laden issued a 'fatwa', or religious edict, declaring that Muslims had the right to fight a 'jihad', or holy war, against Americans and their allies. During the same year, the US embassies of Tanzania and Kenya were bombed, killing over two hundred people and injuring many more. Today, bin Laden is wanted for both these atrocities.

The horror of 9/11

Bin Laden's most bizarre and horrifying terrorist attack was still to come. On 11 September 2001, two hijacked aeroplanes were flown into New York's World Trade Center; a third into the Pentagon; and a fourth crashed into a field in Pennsylvania after passengers resisted the hijackers. The death toll from all the attacks was almost three thousand. After the attacks, bin Laden was named as the prime suspect, but initially denied that he had been involved. He later claimed responsibility for the attacks.

The US government still lacked evidence of his involvement, until a videotape was produced that had apparently been seized by US forces during a raid in Jalalabad. This showed a man who looked like bin Laden discussing how effective the bombing of the World Trade Center had been. The authenticity of the tape has been disputed, but bin Laden's pronouncements since then, and his known involvement in previous terrorist activity, have caused many to believe that he was indeed the mastermind behind 9/11.

On the run

Despite frequent attempts to hunt bin Laden down, the US government has to date failed to apprehend the world's number one terrorist. After the attacks of 2001, the United States invaded Afghanistan, but bin Laden was not found. Some reports suggested that he was dead, either killed in the bombardments or dying from a kidney disorder. At present, bin Laden's whereabouts remain unknown.

Abu Nidal

Before the rise of Osama bin Laden and his organization al-Qaeda, Abu Nidal was one of the most feared terrorists in the western world. A political extremist, he advocated the complete destruction of Israel, and was equally hostile towards Arab moderates who sought to negotiate peace with the Israelis. His organization, the Fatah Revolutionary Council, also known as the Abu Nidal Organization (ANO), carried out a series of attacks – hijackings, shootings, assassinations and bombings – that left hundreds dead and injured, and that led to long, drawn-out hostilities between Arab and Israeli states. The ANO had also, for many years, provided mercenary soldiers for radical Arab regimes. Nidal was supported by several states including Iraq, Libya and Syria, but by the time of his death in 2002, the organization was considerably depleted, with a small base in Iraq and only a few cells remaining in Palestinian refugee camps in Lebanon.

Abu Nidal was born Sabri al-Banna in Jaffa, Israel, in 1937, at a time when Palestine was under British rule. Not a great deal is known about his early life, but he came from a landowning farming family. During the 1948 Arab-Israeli war, his family had to leave their home as a result of the war, and flee to the West Bank. The experience left Nidal with a lifelong hatred of the Israelis.

'Father of struggle'

Nidal's childhood years were spent in Nablus, and he went on to become a teacher. He joined the Ba'ath party in the 1950s and then, in 1967, the Palestine Liberation Organization (PLO). He adopted the name Abu Nidal (meaning 'father of struggle' in Arabic) and identified himself with the radical wing of the party, represented at the time by Yasser Arafat. In 1974, he split from the PLO over political differences. The PLO had proposed the creation of a national authority

A man of many plans – Abu Nidal's organization carried out a huge number of terrorist crimes

The group became the most feared terrorist organization in the world; its targets were not only Jews and supporters of Israel, but moderate Arabs as well.

in the Gaza Strip and the West Bank, as a step towards the setting up of a Palestinian state. However, Nidal felt that this was selling out, and wanted to see continued hostilities towards Israel. He formed his own organization, the Fatah Revolutionary Council (later the ANO). Nidal bitterly opposed any kind of negotiations between the Israeli and Arab world, and was also opposed to moderate Arab regimes. The group became the most feared terrorist organization in the world; its targets were not only Jews and supporters of Israel, but moderate Arabs as well.

During the 1970s and 1980s, Abu Nidal carried out a series of attacks in over twenty countries in Europe, Asia and the Middle East, killing over three hundred people and injuring hundreds more. He was supported by several governments, including Syria, Libya and Iraq, who offered a safe haven to the terrorists. In return, the Fatah Revolutionary Council acted as a mercenary terrorist force for radical Arab regimes. However, these regimes later bowed to international pressure and, to avoid sanctions and political complications, expelled the organization from their territories.

Hijackings and bombings

The attacks carried out by the ANO included two hijackings: the hijacking of EgyptAir Flight 648 in Malta in 1985, which left 58 passengers dead when Egyptian soldiers stormed the plane; and the hijacking of Pan Am Flight 73 in Karachi in 1986. Nidal also masterminded attacks on airports in Rome and Vienna in 1985, leaving twenty dead and more than a hundred injured. Other strikes were the Neve Shalom synagogue in Istanbul during a Sabbath service where twenty-two people were shot dead; and in June 1982, an Israeli Ambassador to Britain was wounded in an attack which resulted in Israel invading Lebanon. This in turn triggered a crisis in relations between Palestine and Israel, in which Israel banished Palestinian troops from its borders.

Further attacks included the killing of nine people and the wounding of ninety-eight on a cruise ship in 1988; and a large car bomb outside the Israeli embassy in Cyprus, which left three dead. In 1991, Abu Iyyad, Arafat's second-in-command, was assassinated in Tunis, along with another PLO official. Three years later, a senior Jordanian diplomat was assassinated in Beirut. In addition, the organization is thought to have killed about a hundred and fifty of its own members as a result of internal purges.

In 2002, news came that Abu Nidal had been shot dead at his home in Baghdad. It was thought that he had committed suicide. He was suffering from leukaemia, and was facing a charge of treason from the Iraqi government. However, other reports suggest that he was shot by Iraqi intelligence agents. Today, the ANO is thought to be based in Iraq, with some support in Lebanon, but it is not thought to be a major international force in the world of terrorism.

Carlos the Jackal

Ilich Ramirez Sanchez, better known as Carlos the Jackal, was once one of the most feared terrorists in the world. During his career of crime, which spanned the 1970s and 1980s, he committed a horrifying series of brutal terrorist attacks across Europe. Most disturbingly, as his trail of carnage increased, he seemed to show that he was no longer fighting for a cause, but was simply enjoying the violence and revelling in his notoriety. He was eventually handed over to the French authorities and imprisoned for life. Today, several cases are still pending against

Carlos the Jackal – a terrorist with a political motivation, or a cruel psychopath killing for the joy of it?

The shocking chaos of the aftermath of an explosion that killed one person and wounded sixty-three – the rue Marbeuf bomb attack, Paris, April 1982, carried out by the Jackal

him, and he has yet to be tried for the majority of the crimes he committed.

Sanchez was born in 1949 in Caracas, Venezuela, the son of a millionaire Marxist lawyer who named his three sons Vladimir, Ilich and Lenin. The young Ilich travelled around the world, picking up skills as a linguist on the way. He later used these as a cover for his activities, posing as a language teacher. As he grew up, he also became involved in youth communist activities. In 1966 his parents divorced, and he moved to London with his mother and brothers.

A bullet in the head

Sanchez went on to study in the Soviet Union, at the Patrice Lumumba University there, where he came into contact with the Communist Party. His interest was in the problems of the Middle East and, at the beginning of the 1970s, he was sent to Amman, Jordan, to train as a guerrilla fighter for the Popular Front for the Liberation of Palestine (PFLP). At this time, he began to use his nickname 'Carlos'. 'The Jackal' was added later, when a copy of the spy thriller *The Day of the Jackal* was found at one of his hide-outs.

After his spell in the Middle East, he returned to London. There, possibly under orders from the PFLP, he performed his first terrorist act. He shot and wounded British businessman Edward Seiff, head of the chain store Marks and Spencer and a major figure in Jewish life. Carlos called on Seiff's house and forced his way in with a gun; it was only by sheer luck that the bullet he put into Seiff's head did not kill the man. During this time, Carlos also launched a bomb attack on an Israeli bank, the Hapoalim Bank, in London.

The Jackal had a stash of weapons with him when the police arrested him in Khartoum, Sudan

Bomb attacks

Carlos then went on to make a series of bomb attacks in France. He bombed the premises of newspaper buildings accused of being pro-Israeli, often making warning calls and arranging for the bombs to be detonated at night, 'to limit casualties', as he said. However, his subsequent attacks in France showed different patterns, and some caused a great deal of damage. In 1982, one person was killed and sixty-three people were injured when a car bomb exploded in the centre of Paris.

His most notorious attack was in 1975, at an Organization of Petroleum Exporting Countries (OPEC) meeting in Vienna, when he led a team of

terrorists who seized over sixty hostages and killed three people. Carlos and his men stormed the meeting, and then demanded that a statement they had written be read out and transmitted by radio all over the Middle East. The terrorists left with their hostages, including ministers from eleven OPEC states. After negotiations with the Austrian government, the hostages were released and the terrorists granted asylum.

From this point, it became clear that Carlos was enjoying his notoriety. The Palestinian groups that had supported him now withdrew their backing. However, Carlos continued to mount terrorist attacks across Europe. Dozens of people were killed and hundreds injured in these attacks.

As his trail of carnage increased, he seemed to show that he was no longer fighting for a cause, but was simply enjoying the violence and revelling in his notoriety.

The killer playboy

During this time, Carlos was harboured by radical Arab regimes in Iraq, Libya, Syria, Yemen and Lebanon. He was protected by the governments of these countries from the agencies that were trying to hunt him down: the CIA, Interpol and French intelligence. As his career continued, it became clear that he was now also acting as a mercenary for these regimes, carrying out attacks at their behest for money. He is thought to have amassed a fortune through this work, and acquired a reputation as a playboy who enjoyed the high life.

In 1982, he and a terrorist group attacked a nuclear reactor in France, but the attempt failed. Two members of the group were arrested, including Carlos' wife Magdalena Kopp, who was connected to the Bader-Meinhof gang in Germany. Carlos wrote to the police asking them to release the pair, and then went on to launch a series of bombings, including one on a passenger train in France, killing five people and injuring dozens more. Despite this attempt to intimidate the authorities, the terrorists were convicted, and Kopp was sentenced to six years' imprisonment. Once she had served her term, she was set free to rejoin Carlos.

Brought to justice

By now it was becoming clear that the Soviet bloc countries were not supporting Carlos' activities any longer. He was also being kept at arm's length by the radical Arab countries. Eventually, Carlos found a home in Syria, but even here he was only allowed to remain on condition that he stop his terrorist activities.

When Iraq invaded Kuwait in 1990, it was rumoured that Saddam Hussein was going to approach Carlos to make terrorist strikes on the United States. Syria expelled Carlos, and he went underground, taking shelter in various Middle Eastern countries. He found his way to the Sudan, which had become a focus for terrorists such as Osama bin Laden. However, his playboy way of life did not sit at all well with the religious fundamentalism of the Islamic sheikh who offered him protection. The sheikh arranged for him to be handed over to the French authorities.

The arrest took place in Khartoum, Sudan, in 1994. Carlos was transferred to France and, after three years of solitary confinement, was tried for three murders – from among the scores that he had committed. He was sentenced to life imprisonment. He staged a short hunger strike, but no one took very much notice, and today he continues to serve out his sentence.

Ted Kaczynski

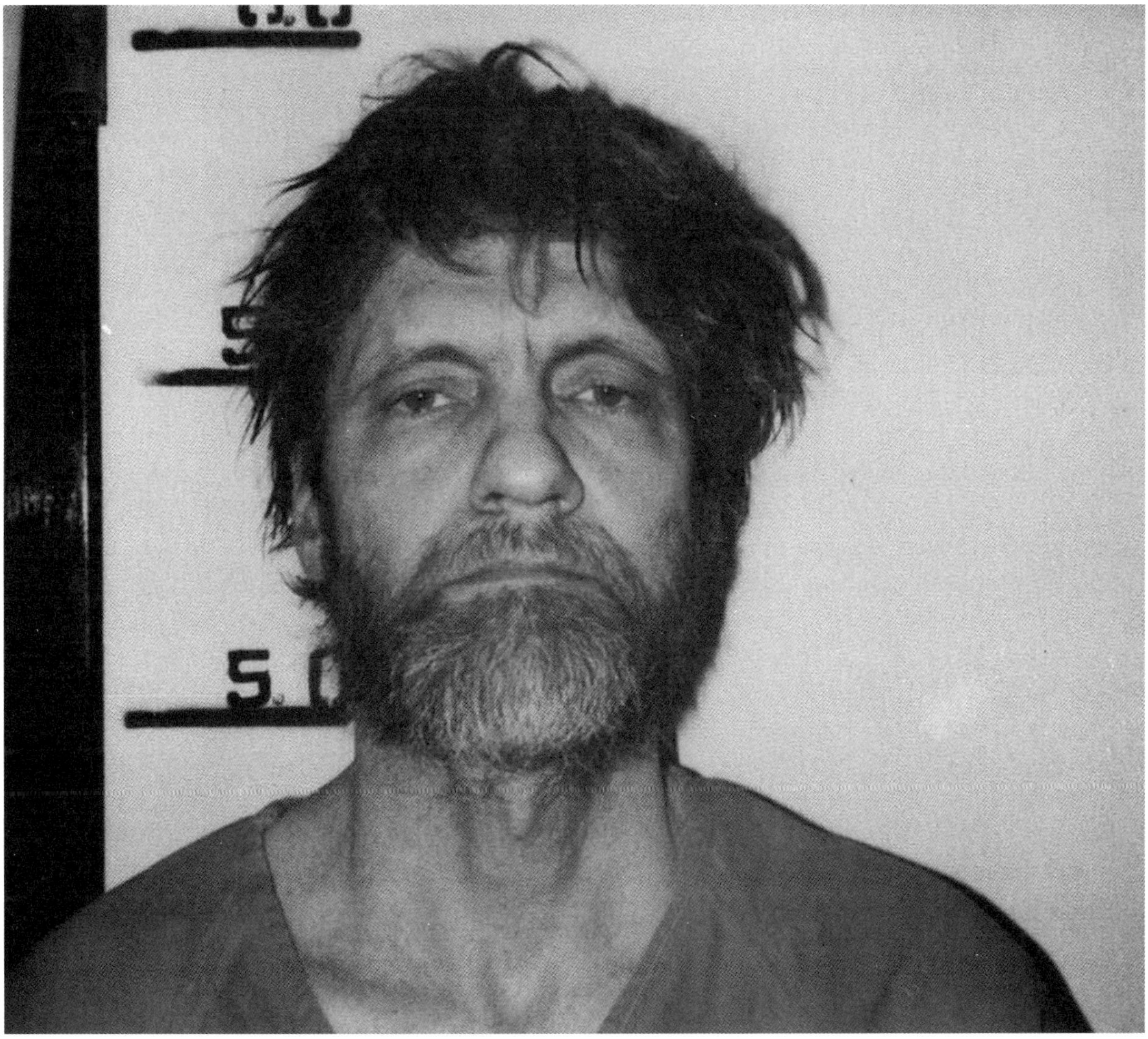

Ted Kaczynski, also known as 'The Unabomber', was a highly intelligent, educated man who nevertheless organized a series of crude bombings that killed and maimed a number of people. He apparently carried out the crimes in the belief that he was helping to cause the downfall of civilized society and halt the progress of technology; but

When put beside those of suave mobsters or white-collar fraudsters, Ted Kaczynski's plans were crude, yet effective

Realizing that his brother was responsible for the bombing campaign, David contacted the police and told them where Ted was living.

it also emerged that, although he had a brilliant academic mind, he was mentally unbalanced.

He was born Theodore John Kaczynski in Chicago on 22 May 1942. He grew up in Evergreen Park, a working-class area in the suburbs of Chicago. While still a baby, he had a strong allergic reaction to some medicine he was given, and had to be taken to hospital. He was kept there for several weeks, separated from his parents, who were only allowed to visit occasionally. His mother attests that, having been a happy baby before the incident, he then became withdrawn and turned away from human contact. It is thought that this separation may have caused him mental health problems later in life.

Mathematics genius

Despite this early setback, Ted showed very high intelligence as a young child, and was clearly very gifted. However, he entirely lacked social skills, and was disinclined to play with other children or to engage with adults. He did well academically, graduating from high school early after skipping several grades. He went on to study mathematics at Harvard, earning his degree there, and then gaining a master's degree and a Ph.D. from Ann Arbor University, Michigan. He astounded his professors with his ability to solve problems they could not, and in a short time reached a level in the subject that only a handful of people in the country would have been able to comprehend. Not surprisingly, he was offered a fellowship and teaching work, and spent three years as a lecturer in Michigan, also publishing papers on mathematics in several learned journals.

Kaczynski was then offered a post at the University of California, Berkeley. He spent two years there as an assistant professor in mathematics, before abruptly resigning from the job in 1969. It was unclear why such a brilliant mathematician, who could have reached the top of his profession in a very short time, suddenly quit the academic scene.

Killer mail bombs

Kaczynski no longer had a permanent source of income, other than the occasional odd jobs he did for local people. His family also helped him out, lending him money. However, he was now extremely poor, and lived in a small cabin in the countryside, isolated from the community and becoming more and more eccentric.

In the late 1970s, Kaczynski began to send bombs through the mail. His first target was a university professor who became suspicious and had the package opened by a campus police officer. It exploded, but fortunately the officer was only slightly injured. Next, Kaczynski began to target airlines, sending bombs designed to explode in airports and on aeroplanes. The bombs were home-made, and not very efficient, so initially little damage was done.

However, Kaczynski then stepped up his campaign with bombs that, while still primitive, were now lethal. In 1985, he sent one to the University of California, which resulted in a student losing four of his fingers and the sight in one eye. In the same year, Kaczynski began to target computer stores, leaving nail bombs in the parking lots outside these stores. In one case, the store owner was killed outright.

The Unabomber manifesto

After this atrocity, Kaczynski's activities ceased for a while. However, in 1993 his next target was a computer science professor at Yale University, David Gelernter, who thankfully survived the bomb Kaczynski mailed to him. Another academic, geneticist Charles Epstein, was not so lucky. He was maimed by one of Kaczynski's bombs in the same year. The following year, Kaczynski targeted an advertising executive, and the year after, the president of the California Forestry Association.

Kaczynski now began to write letters to the papers, and in some cases to his former victims, claiming responsibility for the attacks, on behalf of his 'anarchist group' Freedom Club (FC). He demanded that a manifesto he had written be printed in one of the US's major newspapers and claimed that he would then end his bombing campaign. In order to try to resolve the situation, The *New York Times* printed it, which became known as 'The Unabomber Manifesto'. A great deal of controversy surrounded this decision; in some quarters, it was felt that this was pandering to the murderer. However, the newspaper argued that printing the manifesto might help to solve the mystery of who the Unabomber was, and track the culprit down.

The manifesto was a rant, though at times an intelligent and informed one, against the evils of modern technology. It argued that human beings suffer from the 'progress' of technology, which harms the majority of people on the planet and causes immense environmental damage. Its author believed that the only way forward was through halting technological progress, and returning to the simple life, living close to nature. Kaczynski also criticized 'leftists' for allowing an advanced, complex society to develop to the detriment of humanity.

Closing in on Kaczynski

When the manifesto was published, Kaczynski's brother David recognized it as putting forward Ted's ideas in the writing style he knew only too well. At one time, David had admired his brother greatly, and followed his ideas. In fact, he had bought a plot of land with Ted outside Lincoln in western Montana. Ted now lived there, in a ten by twelve foot cabin without electricity or running water, and led a reclusive life, rarely going out, as his neighbours later reported, except to buy food that he could not grow in his garden. David had baled out from this way of life early on and decided to adopt a more mainstream approach.

Realizing that his brother was responsible for the bombing campaign, David contacted the police and told them where Ted was living. Officers arrested Ted Kaczynski at his cabin in Montana in April 1996. The FBI had assured David that they would not tell his brother who had turned him in, but sadly, his identity was later leaked. David used the reward money he received to pay his legal expenses, but also to recompense the families of his brother's victims.

When the case came to trial, the most obvious defence for Ted Kaczynski was insanity, but Kaczynski rejected this. Instead, a court psychiatrist diagnosed him as fit to stand trial, though suffering from schizophrenia. Kaczynski pleaded guilty to the bombings, but later withdrew his plea. The withdrawal was not accepted, and Kaczynski was given a life sentence with no parole. Today, he continues to serve out his sentence in Florence, Colorado.

Timothy McVeigh

Timothy McVeigh was a terrorist executed by lethal injection for his part in the bombing of the Federal Building of Oklahoma in 1995, which killed 168 people and injured many more. He was the first person to be executed by the state in this way. Although he was portrayed as a mentally unbalanced loner by the media, many believe that he was rational at the time, and that he was acting as part of a wider conspiracy to undermine the government.

McVeigh was born in upstate New York in 1968 and grew up in rural communities near Buffalo, Niagara and Canada. He had two sisters and was the middle child of the family. His father worked in a car factory, and his mother in a travel agency. The marriage was an unhappy one, and the couple separated several times, finally splitting up for good in 1984. As a school pupil, McVeigh was shy and quiet; as a teenager,

Timothy McVeigh was found guilty of the deaths of one hundred and sixty-eight men, women and children in Oklahoma City

A co-worker remembered that he stockpiled guns and food in readiness for the breakdown of 'civilized society'.

he kept to himself and did not socialize much with friends or date girls.

Guns and survivalism

After graduating from high school in 1986, McVeigh went to business college for a short while, living at home with his father and working at Burger King. He then found a job as a security guard in Buffalo, receiving a permit to carry pistols. It was at this time that he became obsessed with guns. He was also beginning to show signs of paranoia, according to the testimony of a co-worker, who remembered that he stockpiled guns and food in readiness for the breakdown of 'civilized society', which he believed was just around the corner. In 1988, he bought a ten-acre plot of land with a friend and began to use it as a shooting range. The same year, he enlisted in the army.

McVeigh became a gunner in the army and did well; he was soon promoted to platoon leader. He spent a great deal of time maintaining his collection of guns, and was interested in politics. He spoke highly of a novel, *The Turner Diaries*, to his army colleagues. The novel is generally regarded as racist and anti-semitic, but there is some controversy as to whether McVeigh himself was actually racist. What is clear is that he had by now adopted a survivalist philosophy, in which he regarded the individual's right to have and use guns as paramount, and the authorities – particularly the US government – as corrupt and evil.

Cold-blooded killing

In 1991, McVeigh's division was sent to the Gulf to take part in the war there. During his time in action, his hatred for the US government increased. He later claimed that he had been ordered to execute surrendering Iraqi prisoners, and that he had witnessed the carnage after the US army had massacred Iraqi soldiers on the road out of Kuwait City. Whatever the truth of the matter, there is no doubt that McVeigh learned to kill without compassion when he was on active service during the Gulf War.

Returning from the Gulf, McVeigh attempted to get into the Special Forces section of the US army, but failed a physical endurance test. The experience left him disappointed and at a loss as to how to advance his career. In 1991, he took advantage of the offer of early discharge from the army and went back home to his father once more. At first he worked as a security guard, as he had done in the past, but he then began to travel around by car, staying in trailer parks and cheap motels, and occasionally visiting his old army buddies around the country.

The Waco fiasco

In 1993, the Waco incident hit the headlines. A cult community known as the Branch Davidians, a religious group that had originated in the Seventh-Day Adventist Church, was targeted by federal agents, who accused the cult members of crimes such as paedophilia. A siege mounted by the authorities ended in the destruction of the cult's compound and the killing of many cult members, including leader David Koresh. Along with many others, McVeigh was incensed by the government's handling of the incident, and went to Waco at the time of the siege to visit the scene.

At around this period, it appears that McVeigh began making bombs. Along with an old army colleague, Terry Nichols, he made a plan to undermine the state government by planting a bomb at the Alfred P. Murrah Federal Building in Oklahoma City. He drove a truck loaded with explosives up to the offices, ignited a timed fuse on the vehicle and then walked away.

The Oklahoma atrocity

The explosives detonated just as the office workers were beginning to open up for business. Children were also arriving at a daycare centre in the building at that time. Having detonated the bomb, McVeigh sped away on the highway out of town, but was arrested for speeding, for driving without a licence and for carrying a concealed weapon. He was nearly released for these minor crimes before being identified as the culprit behind the bombing, after an international manhunt.

In 1997, after a controversial trial, McVeigh was finally convicted of the bombing and sentenced to death. On 11 June 2001, he was executed by lethal injection in Terre Haute Prison, Indiana. His co-conspirator Terry Nichols received a sentence of life imprisonment.

Although McVeigh always assumed sole responsibility for the crime, and the press helped to maintain his image that he was acting alone, many believe that the truth behind the atrocity was somewhat more complex. Some think that McVeigh had other accomplices besides Nichols, including Nichols' brother, James. Others allege that the government itself had a role in the attack, since one report concluded that bombs had been placed within the building itself. According to this far-fetched theory, the government needed grounds for persecuting right-wing groups and thus had a hand in planning the attack in some way.

Terrorist links

More convincing are the theories that McVeigh was operating as part of a larger group. He may have been connected to a criminal group called the Midwest Bank Robbers, who were active in the US in the early 1990s, and who held white supremacist views. The FBI found that the same type of explosive caps were used by both McVeigh and the Robbers, and there was some evidence to show that he and the Robbers had met in Arkansas a short time before the Oklahoma bombing occurred. Another possibility is that McVeigh had met with Islamic fundamentalist terrorists in the Philippines not long before the attack, and may have been linked to the al-Qaeda network.

Whatever the truth of the matter, Timothy McVeigh will go down in history as the biggest American mass murderer. The Oklahoma City bombing was an atrocity that shocked the nation and the world, not only because of the sheer scale of the attack, but also because it was so random in nature, killing innocent victims, most of them civilians, and some of them children and babies.

Index

Bibliography

Abagnale, Frank William, Jr. with Redding, Stan, *Catch Me if You Can,* First Broadway Books, 2000.

Bergen, Peter L. *Holy War, Inc: Inside the Secret World of Osama bin Laden*, Free Press, 2001.

Bugliosi, Vincent, with Gentry, Curt, *Helter Skelter: The True Story of the Manson Murders,* Bantam, 1995.

Boyle, Andrew, *The Fourth Man,* Dial, 1979.

Deacon, Richard, *The Cambridge Apostles: A History of Cambridge University's Elite Intellectual Secret Society,* Farrar, Strauss & Giroux, 1986.

Cyriax, Oliver, *Crime: An Encyclopedia*, Andre Deutch, 1993.

Irving, Clifford, *Fake! The Story of Elmyr de Hory, the Greatest Art Forger of Our Time,* McGraw-Hill, 1969.

Knightley, Phillip, *The Second Oldest Profession,* Andre Deutsch, 1986.

Longrigg, Clare, *Mafia Women*, Vintage, 1998.

McMenomy, Keith, *Ned Kelly: The Authentic Illustrated Story,* Currey O'Neil Ross, 1984.

Morton, James, *Gangland*, Little Brown, 1992.

Naifeh, Steven and White Smith, Gregory, *The Mormon Murders*, New American Library, 1988.

Pearson, John, *The Profession of Violence*, Weidenfeld & Nicolson, 1972.

Reeve, Simon, *The New Jackals: Ramzi Yousef, Osama Bin Laden and the Future of Terrorism,* Northeastern University Press, 1999.

Schoenberg, Robert J., *Mr Capone: The Real and Complete Story of Al Capone,*William Morrow, 1992.

Toland, John, *The Dillinger Days,* Random House, 1963.

Wallis, Michael, *Pretty Boy: The Life and Times of Charles Arthur Floyd,* St.Martin's Press, 1992.

West, Nigel, ed., *The Faber Book of Espionage,* Faber, 1995.

Wright, Peter, *Spycatcher.* Viking, 1987.

Acknowledgments

Illustrations reproduced with the kind permission of the following:

AKG
Pages: 101, 102

Corbis
Pages: 27, 31, 38, 40, 58, 57, 60, 69, 106, 120, 127, 130, 134, 145, 163, 164

Getty Images
Pages: 59, 62, 66, 73, 79, 108, 110, 116, 120, 155, 170, 172, 177, 185

Kobal Collection (Picture Desk)
Pages: 32, 43, 56, 179

Rex
Pages: 46, 47, 52, 64, 71, 76, 90, 93, 96, 99, 113, 114, 133, 137, 139, 175, 191, 193, 196, 201

Topfoto
Pages: 12, 13, 14, 16, 17, 18, 20, 22, 23, 35, 45, 51, 55, 61, 67, 74, 75, 81, 83, 87, 88, 104, 109, 117, 119, 123, 125, 135, 140, 142, 144, 147, 149, 150, 151, 152, 153, 157, 158, 160, 167, 168, 169, 182, 185, 195, 199, 204

Front cover
Topfoto and Getty images